THE ULTIMATE LEAN AND GREEN COOKBOOK

Get in Shape Weight 5&1 Plan | Includes Delicious Low-Carb Fuelings for Beginners, Ready in Under 30 Minutes

Stacey Matthews

About Stacey Matthews

Writing a book can be the most challenging task only aspiring authors will complete it. With profound thinking, pursuing their vision and goals, sharpening their focus, respecting their time, and planning strategically, they are able to write such a masterpiece that brings revolutionary changes in the lives of people. Stacey Matthews is one of them with a strong passion and desire to make a difference in people's lives as she shares an opinion that the world would be a happier, healthier, more human place if everyone follow the proper nutrition plan or instruction of a nutritionist.

Stacey Matthews is a writer, nutritionist, recovery coach, and consultant who is dedicated to assisting others that a healthy diet is a crucial part of staying healthy and is essential for maintaining the body. In her books, she provides realistic and honest guidance so that their readers get the most out of reading her work. she shares her personal experience made on her skin, academic and independent studies as well as gives complete scientific backed information to help even ablute beginners benefit from her books.

Forty-three years Stacey Matthews graduated in Nutrition and Dieting from a prestigious university. In her childhood, she was obese and grown-up bullied for her appearance, which became a sensitive spot for her. It made her feel humble about herself, and she wanted to turn her life around. And that's where proper nutrition come in which she experiences during her weight loss journey and wants her readers to learn from her experience.

Stacey Matthews is also a mental coach as she believes that a mental approach is more important to losing weight. Her books will help the readers finally discover the most natural and efficient way for their bodies to lose weight without giving up the taste of the foods they love.

If you are looking to have more control over your health, let " Stacey Matthews books" show the way.

Table of Contents

PART 4-SNACKS

CHAPTER 10.   MORNING SNACKS

CHAPTER 11.   AFTERNOON SNACKS

CHAPTER 12.   AFTER- DINNER SNACKS

CHAPTER 13.   SHOPPING LIST

CONCLUSION

Introduction

Dear reader, this amazing cookbook will serve as your faithful companion on your journey to the physical transformation you've always dreamed of having.

But before you work your way through the kitchen, you need to immediately understand the concept of what lies behind your desire to get healthy again and the reasons why you bought this cookbook, so that you can pursue a targeted workout plan to achieve your goal.

You know, you hear all kinds of things about health; diets pop up every year like new fads, exactly as if they were clothes for a wardrobe makeover; understanding why you chose to commit to the program in this book is, therefore, essential to not give up at the first difficulties. Being aware that you will encounter some is essential to not giving up and not having wasted your money on this writing.

Therefore, I would like you to immediately take a blank sheet of paper and write down first of all what is the real motivation that prompted you to make this important decision to buy my book: be honest with yourself, and above all, do not judge this reason.

This introspective work will help you understand the real reason why you resort to overeating or junk food.

Once you understand this, you will see it will be easier because you will have a clear understanding of who and what you are doing it for, keeping in mind that any great accomplishment takes time, perseverance and dedication.

In this way, you will not only get external results, but you will also be a renewed person internally, able to listen to yourself and understand how to deal with the problems that life puts in front of you, thus also increasing your self-esteem and self-love.

As you may have already guessed, this cookbook is designed to make you lose weight in a steady and targeted way, in a naturally progressive way, avoiding structural and aesthetic damage such as sagging skin and irritability from diets that are carried on for too long, even years, making them unsustainable for a person who needs positive feedback.

A big mistake that usually falls is to fixate on looking at calorie counting charts instead of focusing solely on weighing food with dedication.

This is not what I want to teach you, because these habits put you in a mental state of anxiety and stress and above all they are useless, as it is not the number of calories: that should be put in the foreground, but the quality of the food as much as possible. Fresh, vital and whole to eat without obsession; weighing food is the only precaution you need to take only as a guideline, but they should not become your prison, especially at the end when you follow 3 & 3 because they take you away from your comfort zone, which is essential to feel good physically and mentally.

So, focus only on the things that get you results without stress, while for the details, you always have time to apply them in the future; don't forget that you have a myriad of recipes to try and try again.

One key thing is the shopping list: I've been focusing a lot on this and I want you to understand the importance of this tool that everyone ignores and underestimates by putting it on the back burner. If you plan your shopping list, you'll magically find yourself spending less money and reclaiming a lot of time with just 10 minutes of evening work before going to the supermarket. And you won't be distracted by what you have to choose from once you enter your local supermarket.

In addition, to help you even more, I have divided the cookbook into three distinct parts to test your tastes (omnivore, vegetarian and vegan) from here you can choose according to the stage you are in 5&1 and 4&2&1 with recipes without the use of dairy, cheese, legumes and the 3&3 section to restore everything with the right precautions, all chronologically divided according to the number of people to whom the recipe is addressed, but don't worry because you'll just have to take a look at the Lean and Green breakdown in order to keep an eye on the daily score so, you'll find your balance.

Don't forget the snacking section of the book: these are the secret recipes for burning fat with the power of metabolism by always trying to eat the six daily meals.

If as you progress with your results you feel you no longer need all that food, you can always lower the amounts I put in each recipe and eliminate the sixth snack meal after dinner.

OMNIVOROUS

Breakfast recipes

1. Breakfast Burrito

Preparation Time: 15 minutes
Cooking Time: 10 minutes
Servings: 2
L & G Counts: 3 condiments, 1 lean, 3 green, 1 healthy fat
Ingredients:

- 2 medium Eggs
- 4 medium Egg Whites
- 2 tbsp Whole Flax Seeds
- 3 dash Light Cooking Spray
- 4 oz Reduced-Fat Pepper Jack Cheese Shredded
- 2 cup Baby Spinach Chopped
- 1 cup Tomatoes Diced
- 1/2 cup Green Bell Peppers Diced
- 1 medium Jalapeno Peppers Diced
- 1 tbsp Red Onion Chopped
- 1 tsp Garlic Cloves Minced
- 2 tsp Balsamic Vinegar
- 1/8 tsp Salt (optional)
- 1/8 tsp Black Pepper
- 1/4 cup Fresh Cilantro Chopped

Directions:

1. In a small bowl, whisk the ingredients for the tortilla (2 eggs, 4 egg whites and 2 tablespoons of flaxseed)
2. Heat a small skillet over medium heat and lightly grease it with cooking spray. Pour half of the egg mixture into the pan and spread the eggs evenly over the surface, forming a thin tortilla or crepe-like shape. Fry for a few minutes until the edges and bottom of the tortilla are firm. Tilt the pan from side to side to make sure the eggs are no longer runny. Carefully loosen the tortilla from the surface with a spatula and turn it gently. Continue cooking until the eggs are completely set. Repeat the process with the other half of the tortilla mixture. Set the tortillas aside when they're done.
3. Lightly grease the same pan and sauté the spinach over low to medium heat for 2 to 3 minutes, until wilted. When cooked, remove from heat and set aside.
4. Mix all ingredients for the salsa in a medium bowl (diced tomatoes, bell peppers, jalapenos, red onions, garlic, balsamic vinegar, salt, bell pepper and cilantro)
5. Place the tortilla on a large plate. Place half of the spinach, cheese and salsa in the center, then roll up into a burrito. Serve immediately.

Nutrition: Calories: 273 Fat: 7g Carbohydrates: 16g Protein: 23g

2. Tuna Spinach Casserole

Preparation Time: 30 minutes
Cooking Time: 25 minutes
Servings: 8
L & G Counts: 2 leans ,1 green, 0 healthy fat, 0 condiment
Ingredients:

- 18 ounces mushroom soup, creamy
- ½ cup milk
- 12 ounces white tuna, solid, in water, drained
- 8 ounces crescent dinner rolls, refrigerated
- 8 ounces egg noodles, wide, uncooked
- 8 ounces cheddar cheese, shredded
- 9 ounces spinach, chopped, frozen, thawed, drained
- 2 teaspoons lemon peel grated

Directions:

6. Preheat the oven to 350 degrees Fahrenheit.
7. Lightly coat a glass baking dish in cooking spray (11x7-inch).
8. Cook and drain the noodles as directed on the package.
9. In a skillet heated on medium, combine the cheese (½ cup) and soup. When the cheese has melted, add the noodles, milk, spinach, tuna, and lemon peel. Pour into the prepared dish once it has begun to bubble.
10. Unroll the dough and top with the remaining cheese (½ cup). To seal the dough, roll it up and pinch the edges. Cut the tuna mixture into eight pieces and serve with it.
11. Cook everything in the air fryer for 20 to 25 minutes.

Nutrition: Calories: 400 Fat: 10g Carbohydrates: 30g Protein: 20g

3. Green Goddess Dressing with Grilled Chicken Power Bowl

Preparation Time: 5 minutes
Cooking Time: 15 minutes
Servings: 4
L & G Counts: 3 condiments, 1 lean, 3 green, 0 healthy fat
Ingredients:

- 1 ½ boneless, skinless chicken breasts
- ¼ teaspoon each salt & pepper
- 1 cup rice or kabocha squash cubes
- 1 cup diced zucchini
- 1 cup yellow summer squash
- 1 cup rice broccoli
- 8 cherry tomatoes, halved
- 4 radishes, sliced thin
- 1 cup shredded red cabbage
- ¼ cup hemp or pumpkin seeds

Green Goddess Dressing:

- ½ cup plain Greek yogurt (low-fat)
- 1 cup fresh basil
- 1 clove garlic
- 4 tablespoon lemon juice
- ¼ teaspoon each salt & pepper

Directions:

1. Heat the oven to 350°F.Season the chicken to taste with salt and pepper.
2. Bake for 12 minutes, or until the chicken reaches 165°F. Remove from the oven and set aside for 5 minutes to rest. Keep warm by cutting into bite-sized pieces.
3. Steam riced kabocha squash, yellow summer squash, zucchini, and broccoli in a covered microwave-safe bowl for about 5 minutes, or until tender.
4. To make the dressing, puree all of the ingredients until smooth in a blender.
5. To serve, divide the Veggie Mix evenly among four individual bowls. Add a quarter of the chicken and a tablespoon of seeds to each bowl, along with an equal amount of cherry tomatoes, radishes, and chopped cabbage. Get dressed up. Enjoy!

Nutrition: Calories: 300 Protein: 43 g Carbohydrate: 12 g Fat: 10 g

4. Protein Muffins

Preparation Time: 10 minutes
Cooking Time: 15 minutes
Servings: 12
L & G Counts: 1 leans ,0 green, 1 healthy fat , 1 condiment
Ingredients:

- 8 eggs
- 2 a spoonful of vanilla protein powder
- 8 ounces cream cheese
- 4 tablespoons butter, melted

Directions:

1. Combine cream cheese and melted butter in a large mixing bowl.
2. Whisk in the eggs and protein powder until well combined.
3. Fill muffin cups with the batter.
4. Bake at 350°F for 25 minutes.
5. Serve and enjoy.

Nutrition: 149 Calories: 12g, Fat: 8g Protein:20g

5. Bacon-Wrapped Fried Egg

Difficulty: Easy
Preparation Time: 5 minutes
Cooking Time: 10 minutes
Servings: 1
L & G Counts : 2 leans ,0 green, 1 healthy fat , 2 condiment
Ingredients:

- 30 grams bacon
- 2 eggs
- Salt
- Pepper
- Olive oil (2 Tbsp.)

Directions:

1. Heat the oil in the pan before frying the bacon.
2. Remove the pan from the heat and whisk the eggs in it.
3. Cook the eggs with pepper and salt to taste.
4. Finally, serve the cooked eggs with the bacon hot.

Nutrition: Protein: 19g, Calories: 405, Fat: 38g

6. Avocado Chicken Salad

Preparation Time: 5 minutes
Cooking Time: 10 minutes
Servings: 2
L & G Counts: 3 lean meats, 2 green vegetables, 1 healthy fat, and 2 condiments
Ingredients:

- ¼ cup fresh cilantro, chopped
- 10 ounces diced cooked chicken
- 3 ounce chopped avocado
- 1 tablespoon + 1 tsp lime juice
- ½ cup 2% Plain Greek yogurt
- ¼ teaspoon salt
- 12 teaspoon garlic powder
- 1 tsp Pepper

Directions:

1. Mix all components in an ovenproof dish and refrigerate until serving.
2. Cut the chicken salad in half and serve with your preferred greens.

Nutrition: Fat: 13g, Protein: 35g, Calories: 265

7. Beef and Broccoli in Rice

Preparation Time: 5 minutes
Cooking Time: 15 minutes
Servings: 2
L & G Counts: 2 leans ,1 green, 1 healthy fat, 3 condiment
Ingredients:

- 1 tablespoon + 2 teaspoons low sodium soy sauce
- 1 Splenda packet
- 1 teaspoon sesame or olive oil
- 1 pound raw beef round steak, cut into strips.
- 1 ½ cup broccoli florets
- ½ cup water
- 2 cup cooked, grated cauliflower

Directions:

1. Season the steak with soy sauce and set aside for about 15 minutes.
2. Heat the oil over medium heat and stir-fry the meat for 3-5 minutes
3. Stir in the Splenda, broccoli, and water. Stir for 5 minutes, or until the broccoli begins to soften.
4. Return the meat to the pan and heat it thoroughly.
5. Serve alongside cauliflower rice.

Nutrition: Fat: 4g, Calories: 201, Protein: 23g

8. Chicken Chili

Difficulty: Average
Preparation Time: 10 minutes
Cooking Time: 30 minutes
Servings: 1
L & G Counts: 1 lean, 2 green, 1 good fat, 3 condiments
Ingredients:

- 1(¼ pound) boneless chicken breast
- ¼ tablespoon olive oil
- ¼ cup green spring onion, diced
- 1/3 cup bell pepper, seeded and chopped
- ½ cup jalapenos, seeded and diced
- ½ cloves garlic, minced
- ½ teaspoon salt
- ¼ teaspoon ground cumin
- ¼ teaspoon coriander
- 1 cup chicken broth
-
- ½ cup water
- ½ (7-oz.) cans green chilies
- 1 garnish with a tablespoon of thick canned coconut milk, chopped green onions, and coriander

Directions:

1. Finely chop the chicken and vegetables. Then, in a large pot, heat the oil over medium-high heat. Place the peppers, oil, onions, jalapeno, and garlic in a mixing bowl.
2. After 5 minutes, add the chicken, spices and salt. Cook for another 5 to 8 minutes, until the chicken is fully cooked.
3. In a mixing bowl, combine the green chilies, broth, and coconut milk.
4. Heat to a boil. Cook for 15–20 minutes before shredding the chicken. Garnish with green onions and coriander.

Nutrition: Calories: 226, Protein: 20g, Fat: 8g

9. Roasted Garlic Bacon and Potatoes

Preparation Time: 5 minutes
Cooking Time: 25 minutes
Servings: 4
L & G Counts: 1 lean ,2 green, 1 healthy fat, 3 condiment
Ingredients:

- 3 lb Medium-sized potatoes
- 1 Strip streaky bacon
- 2 tablespoons Sprigs Rosemary
- ½ Cloves garlic unpeeled smashed,
- 3 teaspoon vegetable oil

Directions:

1. Heat the Air Fryer to 390°F.
2. In a mixing bowl, combine the smashed garlic, bacon, potatoes, rosemary, and oil. Stir everything together thoroughly.
3. Place in the air fryer basket and bake for 25 minutes, or until golden brown.

Nutrition: Calories: 114 Fat: 8.1g Protein: 6.2g

10. Stuffed Meatballs

Preparation Time: 10 minutes
Cooking Time: 10 minutes
Servings: 4
L & G Counts: 1 lean, 2 green, 1 good fat, 3 condiments
Ingredients:

- 1/3 cup bread crumbs
- 2 tablespoons milk
- 1 tablespoon ketchup
- 1 Egg
- ½ teaspoon marjoram, dried
- Season with salt and black pepper to taste
- 1-pound Lean beef, ground
- 20 Cheddar cheese cubes
- 1 tablespoon olive oil

Directions:

1. In a mixing bowl, combine the breadcrumbs, ketchup, milk, marjoram, salt, pepper, and egg.
2. Stir in the beef and form 20 meatballs with it.
3. Wrap each meatball in a cube of cheese and coat with oil and rub.
4. Cook the patties for 10 minutes at 390°F in a preheated air fryer.
5. Serve with a side salad for lunch.

Nutrition: Calories: 112 Fat: 8.2g Protein: 7.7g

Lunch Recipes

11. Crab Cakes

Preparation Time: 20 minutes
Cooking Time: 10 minutes
Servings: 2
L & G Counts: 1 lean ,1 green, 1 healthy fat, 3 condiment
Ingredients:

- ½ pound lump crabmeat, drained
- 2 a couple of tablespoons of coconut flour
- 1 tablespoon mayonnaise
- ¼ teaspoon green Tabasco sauce
- 3 a pound of butter
- 1 small egg, beaten
- ¾ tablespoon fresh parsley, chopped
- ½ teaspoon mustard, yellow
- Salt and black pepper, to taste

Directions:

1. In a bowl, combine the ingredients except the butter.
2. Make patties from this mixture and set them aside.
3. Heat butter in a skillet over medium heat and add patties.
4. Cook for about 10 minutes on each side and dish out to serve hot.
5. For meal prep, you can freeze the raw patties for about 3 weeksPlace the patties in a container, spacing them apart to prevent them from sticking together.

Nutrition: Calories: 153 Fat: 10.8g Carbs: 6.7g Protein: 6.4g Sugar: 2.4 Sodium: 46mg

12. Flavorful Taco Soup

Preparation Time: 5 minutes
Cooking Time: 15
Servings: 8
L & G Counts : 1 leans ,0 green, 0 healthy fat , 2 condiment
Ingredients:

- 1 pound ground beef
- 3 tablespoons taco seasoning, divided
- 4 cups beef bone broth
- 2 14.5-oz cans diced tomatoes
- 3/4 cup Ranch dressing

Directions:

1. Brown ground beef in a saucepan over medium-high heat for about 10 minutes.
2. Combine 3/4 cup broth and 2 tablespoons taco seasoning in a mixing bowl. Cook until most of the liquid has evaporated.
3. Add the diced tomatoes, the remaining broth, and the remaining taco seasoning to the pot. Stir to combine, then reduce to a low heat for ten minutes.
4. Remove from the heat and stir in the ranch dressing. As an accompaniment, serve with cilantro and cheddar cheese.

Nutrition: Calories: 309 Fat: 24g Protein: 13g

13. Beet Greens with Pine Nuts Goat Cheese

Preparation Time: 25 minutes
Cooking Time: 15 minutes
Servings: 3
L & G Counts : 1 leans ,1 green, 2 healthy fat , 1 condiment
Ingredients:

- 4 cups beet tops, washed and chopped roughly
- 1 teaspoon EVOO
- 1 tablespoon no sugar added balsamic vinegar
- 2 ounces crumbled dry goat cheese
- 2 tablespoons toasted pine nuts

Directions:

5. Warm the oil in a pan, then cook the beet greens on medium-high heat until they release their moisture. Cook until almost tender. Season with salt and pepper and remove from heat.
6. Toss the greens in a mixture of balsamic vinegar and olive oil, then top with the nuts and cheese. Serve warm.

Nutrition: Calories: 215 Total Carbohydrate: 4 g Cholesterol: 12 mg Total Fat: 18 g Fiber: 2 g Protein:10g

14. Lemon Tilapia Parmesan

Preparation Time: 12 minutes
Cooking Time: 15 minutes
Servings: 3
L & G Counts : 1 leans ,1 green, 1 healthy fat , 2 condiment
Ingredients:

- 1 ½ pound of tilapia fillet or codfish fillet
- 2 tablespoons olive oil
- 2 cloves garlic, minced
- Salt and ground black pepper
- 2 cayenne pepper dashes
- 1 ½ tablespoon lemon juice
- ½ cup Parmesan cheese, shredded

Directions:

1. Pat dries the tilapia fillet with a paper towel and season it with, cayenne pepper, lemon juice, minced garlic, olive oil, salt, and black pepper.
2. Grease the basket of the air fryer with cooking spray.
3. Place the fish in the basket of the air fryer.
4. Place the basket inside the unit.
5. For 15 minutes, use AIRFRY mode at 350°F.
6. When finished, top with cheese and serve.

Serving Suggestion: Serve with wedges of lime.
Variation Tip: Use hard cheese for sprinkling.
Low Nutrition Per Serving: Calories: 414| Fat: 17.5g| Sodium: 15064mg | Carbs: 1.9g | Fiber: 0.1g | Sugar: 0.2g | Protein: 68.9g

15. Chicken with Avocado Salsa

Preparation Time: 15 minutes
Cooking Time: 22 minutes
Servings: 6
L & G Counts : 2 leans ,1 green, 1 healthy fat , 2 condiment
Ingredients:
Chicken Ingredients:

- 2 pounds raw skinless chicken
- 1/3 cup cilantro, chopped
- 2 clove garlic
- ½ teaspoon Cumin
- 2 tablespoons lime juice
- 2 teaspoons vegetable oil
- Salt and black pepper, to taste

Salsa Ingredients:

- 1 cup tomatoes, chopped
- 2 avocados, pitted and chopped
- 2 teaspoons red onion
- 1 teaspoon lime juice
- Salt and black pepper, to taste
- ¼ teaspoon pepper

Directions:

1. Mix the cilantro, garlic, lime juice, salt, cumin, and vegetable oil in a bowl, and marinate the chicken in it by coating the chicken well with the mixture.
2. Preheat the air fryer for 10 minutes at 390°F
3. Afterward, bake the chicken in the air fryer at 390°F for 22 minutes.
4. Remember to flip the chicken halfway through.
5. Mix well all the salsa ingredients in a bowl and serve it with chicken.

Serving Suggestion: Serve with it steamed vegetables
Variation Tip: None
Nutritional Information Per Serving: Calories: 447| Fat: 25.9g| Sodium: 137mg | Carbs: 7.8g | Fiber: 5g | Sugar: 1.3g | Protein: 45.4g

16. Tilapia with Green Beans

Preparation Time: 15 minutes
Cooking Time: 12 minutes
Servings: 2
L & G Counts : 2 leans ,1 green, 1 healthy fat , 2 condiments
Ingredients:

- 2 tilapia fillets, 4 ounces each
- 2 teaspoons olive oil
- 2 teaspoons smoked paprika
- Salt and black pepper, to taste
- 1 cup broccoli
- 2 tablespoons lemon juice
- 1 cup green beans
- Oil spray, for greasing

Directions:

1. Season the broccoli and green beans with salt and black pepper after spraying them with oil spray.
2. Rub the salmon fillet with olive oil, smoked paprika, salt, and lemon juice
3. Put the salmon fillets in the basket of the air fryer along with vegetables
4. 4. set the AIRFRY mode to 400°F for 12 minutes.
5. Take out the basket after 7 minutes and transfer the vegetable to the serving plate.
6. When the salmon is done, remove it from the pan and serve with the vegetables.

Serving Suggestion: Serve with mashed potatoes
Variation Tip: None
Nutritional Information Per Serving: Calories: 517 | Fat: 1 3.2g| Sodium: 254mg | Carbs: 8.5g | Fiber: 3.9g | Sugar: 2.1g | Protein: 92.7g

17. Sundried Tomato Salmon

Preparation Time: 20 minutes
Cooking Time: 12 minutes
Servings: 2
L & G Counts : 1 leans ,3 green, 1 healthy fat , 1 condiment
Ingredients:

- 8 ounces raw salmon
- ¼ cup fresh parsley, chopped
- 2 tablespoons Sun-Dried Tomato Dressing
- Oil spray, for greasing
- Salt and black pepper, to taste
- 4 Cherry tomatoes
- 1 cup broccoli, florets

Directions:

7. Preheat the air fryer to 350°F first.
8. In a mixing bowl, combine the parsley, dressing, salt, and pepper, and set aside.
9. Coat the salmon in a bowl mixture and spray it with oil spray.
10. Place the salmon fillets and vegetables in the air fryer basket.
11. Now, set it to 400°F air fry mode for 12 minutes.
12. During the cooking process, baste the salmon twice.
13. When finished, serve.

Serving Suggestion: None
Variation Tip: None
Nutritional Information Per Serving: Calories: 275| Fat: 13g| Sodium: 231mg | Carbs: 18.1g | Fiber: 4.4g | Sugar: 11g | Protein: 25.7g

18. Seared Scallops

Preparation Time: 15 minutes.
Cooking Time: 6 minutes.
Serving: 4
L & G Counts : 1 leans ,1 green, 2 healthy fat , 1 condiment
Ingredients:

- 1 pound large scallops
- Salt, to taste
- Black pepper, to taste
- 1 tablespoon olive oil
- 2 tablespoons butter
- 2 tablespoons parsley, chopped
- Lemon wedges, for serving

Directions:

1. Season all the scallops with salt, black pepper, and oil.
2. Melt the butter in a saucepan and sear the scallops for 3 minutes on both sides.
3. Drizzle parsley on top and garnish with lemon wedges.
4. Serve warm.

Serving Suggestion: Serve the scallops with lemon slices on top.
Variation Tip: Use white pepper for a change of flavor.
Nutritional Information Per Serving: Calories: 378 | Fat: 21g |Sodium: 146mg | Carbs: 7.1g | Fiber: 0.1g | Sugar: 0.4g | Protein: 23g

19.Salad of Shrimp

Preparation Time: 15 minutes.
Cooking Time: 17 minutes.
Serving: 2
L & G Counts : 1 leans ,2 green, 1 healthy fat , 5 condiment
Ingredients:

- 2 tablespoons olive oil
- 1/3 cup red onion, chopped
- 3 cups broccoli slaw
- 3 cups broccoli florets
- 1/2 teaspoon salt
- 2 garlic cloves, minced
- ½ pound shrimp, peeled and deveined
- 1 teaspoon lime juice
- Green onions, chopped, for garnish
- Cilantro, chopped
- Sriracha and red pepper flakes, for garnish

Sesame almond dressing:

- 2 tablespoons almond butter
- 2 tablespoons water
- 1 tablespoon sesame oil
- 1 tablespoon tamari
- 1 tablespoon maple syrup
- 1 teaspoon lime juice
- 1 teaspoon ginger, minced
- 1 clove minced garlic
- 1 teaspoon sriracha sauce
- ¼ teaspoon black pepper

Directions:

1. Mix all the sesame almond dressing in a bowl.
2. Sauté onion with oil in a skillet for 5 minutes.
3. Stir in broccoli slaw and florest then sauté for 7 minutes.
4. Add black pepper and salt, then transfer to a plate.
5. Add minced garlic, shrimp, lime juice, and more oil to the same skillet.
6. Cook for 5 minutes before adding the shrimp and broccoli.
7. Top with the sesame dressing and garnish with cilantro and green onions.
8. Serve warm.

Serving Suggestion: Serve theSalad of Shrimp with cauliflower rice risotto.
Variation Tip: Add paprika for more spice.
Nutritional Information Per Serving: Calories: 212 | Fat: 9g |Sodium: 353mg | Carbs: 8g | Fiber: 3g | Sugar: 4g | Protein: 25g

20. Lamb Cabbage Rolls

Preparation Time: 15 minutes.
Cooking Time: 30 minutes.
Serving: 8
L & G Counts : 2 leans ,2 green,1 healthy fat ,3 condiment
Ingredients:

- ½ cup bulgur, cooked
- 1 large head Savoy cabbage
- 2 tablespoons olive oil
- 2 cups onion, chopped
- 1 cup leeks, chopped
- ¾ teaspoon salt
- ¾ teaspoon black pepper
- ½ teaspoon ground turmeric
- ¼ teaspoon ground ginger
- ¼ teaspoon ground allspice
- 1 pinch ground cinnamon
- 12 ounces ground lamb
- ½ cup parsley, chopped
- 2 teaspoons fresh mint, chopped
- 1 large egg, beaten
- ½ cup white wine
- ½ cup chicken broth
- 2 teaspoons lemon zest, grated
- 3 tablespoons lemon juice

Directions:

1. At 325°F, preheat your oven.
2. Boil cabbage leaves in 2 ½ cups water in a cooking pan and drain.
3. Sauté onion and leeks with oil in a skillet for 8 minutes.
4. Add cinnamon, allspice, ginger, turmeric, black pepper, and salt, then cook for 1 minute.
5. Place the mixture in a bowl and stir in the bulgur.
6. Stir in lamb, parsley, mint, and egg, then mix well.
7. Spread the cabbage leaves o the working surface.
8. Divide the lamb filling at the center of each leaf.
9. Wrap the leaves around the filling and place the wrap in a baking dish.
10. Add lemon juice, lemon zest, broth, and wine around the cabbage rolls.
11. Wrap everything in aluminum foil and bake for 30 minutes.
12. Serve warm.

Serving Suggestion: Serve the rolls with roasted asparagus.
Variation Tip: Add a drizzle of parmesan cheese on top.
Nutritional Information Per Serving: Calories: 391 | Fat: 5g |Sodium: 88mg | Carbs: 3g | Fiber: 0g | Sugar: 0g | Protein: 27g

Dinner Recipes

21. Pan-Seared Beef and Mushrooms

Preparation Time: 15 minutes.
Cooking Time: 17 minutes.
Servings: 4
L & G Counts : 2 leans ,0 green,1 healthy fat ,1 condiment
Ingredients:

- 1 ½ lb. lean beef, cubed
- 1/2 tablespoons Dash Desperation Seasoning
- Nonstick cooking spray
- 4 cups mushrooms, sliced
- 1 cup beef broth
- 1 ½ teaspoon Garlic Gusto Seasoning

Directions:

1. Mix beef with seasoning and sauté in a skillet with cooking spray for 7 minutes.
2. Cook for 10 minutes, stirring occasionally, with the broth and remaining ingredients.
3. Serve warm.

Variation Tip: Drizzle parmesan cheese on top before serving.
Nutritional Information Per Serving: Calories: 255 | Fat: 12g |Sodium: 66mg | Carbs: 13g | Fiber: 2g | Sugar: 4g | Protein: 22g
Serving Suggestion: Serve the beef with sweet potato salad.

22. Lamb Loin Chops with Mustard

Preparation Time: 15 minutes
Cooking Time: 30 minutes
Servings: 4
L & G Counts : 1 leans ,0 green,1 healthy fat ,2 condiment
Ingredients:

- 8 4-ounces lamb loin chops
- 2 tablespoons Dijon mustard
- 1 tablespoon fresh lemon juice
- ½ teaspoon olive oil
- 1 teaspoon dried tarragon
- Salt and black pepper, to taste

Directions:

1. Preheat the Air Fryer to 390°F and lightly grease the Air Fryer basket.
2. In a large mixing bowl, combine the mustard, lemon juice, oil, tarragon, salt, and black pepper.
3. Coat the chops in the mustard mixture and place them in the Air fryer basket.
4. Cook for about 15 minutes, flipping once in between, and serve immediately.

Nutrition: Calories: 433, Fat: 17.6g, Carbohydrates: 0.6g, Sugar: 0.2g, Protein: 64.1g, Sodium: 201mg

23. Lemon & Garlic Chicken

Preparation Time: 30 minutes
Cooking Time: 30 minutes
Servings: 2
L & G Counts : 2 leans ,1 green,2 healthy fat ,3 condiment
Ingredients:

- 4 fresh organic Chicken Legs, Skin on, Thigh included
- 1 large Lemon, sliced into rings (or any other fruit you may wish to use)
- 4 tablespoon Ghee
- 2 tablespoons Coconut or Olive Oil
- 2 tablespoons dried Oregano
- 1 tablespoon dried Rosemary
- 2 tablespoons Fresh Lemon Juice (or other fruit juice if not using Lemon)
- 1 teaspoon smoked and dried Paprika
- 4 cloves minced Garlic
- Sea Salt and freshly cracked Black Pepper, to taste

Directions:

1. Place the ghee, coconut oil, oregano, rosemary, fruit juice, paprika, garlic, salt, and pepper in a food-safe, airtight container such as a zip-lock bag or large glass jar.
2. Add the chicken legs and stir or shake it for a few minutes so the chicken is well covered in marinade.
3. Refrigerate it for at least 30 minutes (or up to 24 hours) to allow the flavors to infuse.
4. Oil the tray or basket of your air fry oven and turn it on to preheat to 350°F.
5. Place the marinated chicken legs in the basket/tray.
6. Place the slices of lemon on and between the chicken legs.
7. Cook for 30 minutes in the air fryer, or until golden brown.
8. Remove the chicken legs in the tray and allow them to stand for 5 to 10 minutes to rest before serving.

Nutrition: Calories: 446; Fat: 26.9 g; Fiber: 2.0 g; Carbs: 4.8 g; Protein: 46 g; Sodium 116 mg

24. Paprika & Pepper Sauce Wings

Preparation Time: 5 minutes
Cooking Time: 20 minutes
Servings: 4
L & G Counts : 1 leans ,0 green,1 healthy fat ,3 condiment
Ingredients:

- 12 chicken wings
- ¼ teaspoon paprika
- ¼ teaspoon garlic powder
- ¼ teaspoon salt
- 1/8 teaspoon black pepper
- ¼ cup cayenne pepper sauce
- ¼ cup unsalted butter

Directions:

1. Preheat the air fryer to 380 degrees Fahrenheit.
2. Wash and dry the chicken wings under running water.
3. Season with salt and pepper to taste, then add the paprika and garlic powder.
4. Place the chicken wings in the air fryer basket and cook for 20 minutes, turning occasionally.Meanwhile, prepare the basting sauce by combining the cayenne pepper sauce and the melted unsalted butter.
5. Using a pastry brush, baste the chicken wings with pepper sauce.
6. Cook for 5 minutes more, or until the pepper sauce caramelizes.
7. Transfer the air-fried chicken wings to a serving platter.

Nutrition: Calories: 385; Fat: 30.5 g; Fiber: 0.4 g; Carbs: 9.8 g; Protein: 17.5 g; Sodium 452 mg

25. Spicy Shrimp Kebab

Preparation Time: 25 minutes
Cooking Time: 20 minutes
Servings: 4
L & G Counts : 1 leans ,1 green,1 healthy fat ,3 condiment
Ingredients:

- 1 ½ pounds jumbo shrimp, cleaned,
- 1 pound cherry tomatoes
- 2 tablespoons butter, melted
- 1 tablespoons sauce
- Sea salt and ground black pepper
- ½ teaspoon oregano
- ½ teaspoon basil
- 1 teaspoon parsley flakes
- ½ teaspoon marjoram
- ½ teaspoon mustard seeds

Directions:

1. Toss all elements in a mixing bowl until the shrimp and tomatoes are covered on all sides.
2. Let the wooden skewers be soaked in water for 15 minutes.
3. Thread the jumbo shrimp and cherry tomatoes onto skewers. Cook in the preheated air fryer at a temperature of 400°F for 5 minutes, working with batches.

Nutrition: Calories: 247, Fat: 8.4g, Carbohydrates: 6g, Protein: 36.4g, Sugar: 3.5g, Fiber: 1.8g

26. Crumbed Fish Fillets with Tarragon

Preparation Time: 25 minutes
Cooking Time: 20 minutes
Servings: 4
L & G Counts : 2 leans ,0 green,1 healthy fat ,3 condiment
Ingredients:

- 2 eggs, beaten
- ½ teaspoon tarragon
- 4 fish fillets, halved
- 2 tablespoons dry white wine
- 1/3 cup parmesan cheese, grated
- 1 teaspoon seasoned salt
- 1/3 teaspoon mixed peppercorns
- ½ teaspoon fennel seed

Directions:

1. Add the parmesan cheese, salt, peppercorns, fennel seeds, and tarragon to your food processor; blitz for about 20 seconds.
2. Drizzle fish fillets with dry white wine. Dump the egg into a shallow dish.
3. Now, coat the fish fillets with the beaten egg on all sides; then, coat them with the seasoned cracker mix.
4. Air-fry at 345°F for about 17 minutes.

Nutrition: 305 Calories: 17.7g fat 6.3g Carbohydrates 27.2g protein 0.3g sugars 0.1g fiber

27. Sriracha & Honey Tossed Calamari

Preparation Time: 10 minutes
Cooking Time: 20 minutes
Servings: 2
L & G Counts : 1 leans ,0 green,0 healthy fat ,4 condiment
Ingredients:

- 1 cup Club soda
- 1-2 tablespoons Sriracha
- 2 cups Calamari tubes
- 1 cup Flour
- Pinches salt, freshly ground black pepper, red pepper flakes, and red pepper
- 1/2 cup Honey

Directions:

1. Make rings out of calamari tubes. Using club soda, submerge them. Allow for a ten-minute rest period.
2. Meanwhile, combine freshly ground black pepper, flour, red pepper, and kosher salt in a mixing bowl.
3. Drain and dry the calamari with a paper towel. Set aside the calamari after thoroughly coating it in the flour mixture.
4. Spray the air fryer basket with oil and arrange the calamari in a single layer.
5. Cook at 375°F for 11 minutes. Toss the rings twice while cooking. Meanwhile, make the sauce with honey, red pepper flakes, and sriracha in a bowl, well mix.
6. Take calamari out from the basket, mix with sauce, cook for another 2 minutes more.
1. Serve with salad green.

Nutrition: Cal 252 Fat: 38g Carbs: 3.1g Protein: 41g

28. Roasted Salmon with Fennel Salad

Preparation Time: 15 minutes
Cooking Time: 10 minutes
Servings: 4
L & G Counts : 1 leans ,1 green,1 healthy fat ,4 condiment
Ingredients:

- 4 salmon fillets, Skinless and center-cut
- 1 teaspoon Lemon juice (fresh)
- 2 teaspoons Parsley (chopped)
- 1 teaspoon salt, divided
- 2 tablespoons Olive oil
- 1 teaspoon Chopped thyme
- 4 cups Fennel heads (thinly sliced)
- 1 clove minced garlic
- 2 tablespoons Fresh dill, chopped
- 2 tablespoons Orange juice (fresh)
- 2/3 cup Greek yogurt (reduced-fat)

Directions:

1. Combine half a teaspoon of salt, parsley, and thyme in a mixing bowl. Drizzle oil over the salmon and top with the thyme mixture.
2. Put salmon fillets in the air fryer basket, cook for ten minutes at 350°F.
3. Meanwhile, in a mixing bowl, combine the garlic, fennel, orange juice, yogurt, half teaspoon of salt, dill, and lemon juice.
4. Serve with fennel salad.

Nutrition: Calories: 36 Fat: 30g Protein: 38g Carbohydrate 9g

29. Chicken Goulash

Preparation Time: 10 minutes
Cooking Time: 17 minutes
Servings: 6
L & G Counts : 1 leans ,2 green,1 healthy fat ,3 condiment
Ingredients:

- 4 ounces chive stems
- 2 chopped green peppers
- 1 teaspoon olive oil
- 14 ounces ground chicken
- 2 tomatoes
- ½ cup chicken stock
- 2 garlic cloves, sliced
- 1 teaspoon salt
- 1 teaspoon black pepper, ground
- 1 teaspoon mustard

Directions:

1. Chop chives roughly.
2. Spray the air fryer basket tray with olive oil.
3. Preheat the air fryer to 365 degrees Fahrenheit. Fill the air fryer basket tray halfway with chopped chives.
4. Add the chopped green pepper and cook the vegetables for 5 minutes. Add the ground chicken.
5. Cube the tomatoes and combine them with the air fryer mixture.
6. Cook the mixture for 6 more minutes.
7. Add the chicken stock, sliced garlic cloves, salt, ground black pepper, and mustard.
8. Mix well. Cook the goulash for 6 more minutes. Serve and enjoy.

Nutrition: Calories: 161 Fat: 6.1 g Carbs: 6 g Protein: 20.3 g

30. Mussels Mariniere

Preparation Time: 10 minutes
Cooking Time: 30 minutes
Serving: 4
L & G Counts : 0 leans ,0 green,1 healthy fat ,3 condiment
Ingredients:

- 2 tablespoons unsalted butter
- 1 leek
- 1 shallot
- 2 cloves garlic
- 2 bay leaves
- 1 cup white wine
- 2 pounds mussels
- 2 tablespoons mayonnaise
- 1 tablespoon lemon zest
- 2 tablespoons parsley
- 1 sourdough bread

Directions:

1. Melt butter in a saucepan, then add leeks, garlic, bay leaves, and shallot and cook until the vegetables are soft.
2. Bring the water to a boil, then add the mussels and cook for 1–2 minutes.
3. Place mussels in a bowl and cover.
4. Return mussels to pot and whisk in remaining butter and mayonnaise.
5. Stir in the lemon juice, parsley, and zest of the lemon.
6. Plate and serve.

Nutrition: Calories: 321 Total Carbohydrate: 2 g Cholesterol: 13 mg Total Fat: 17 g Fiber: 2 g Protein: 9g Sodium: 312 mg

VEGETARIANS

Breakfast Recipes

31. Hash Browns

Preparation Time: 15 minutes
Cooking Time: 15 minutes
Servings: 4
L & G Counts : 0 leans ,0 green,1 healthy fat ,2 condiment
Ingredients:

- 1 pound russet potatoes, peeled, processed using a grater
- Pinch sea salt
- Pinch black pepper, to taste
- 3 tablespoon Olive oil

Directions:

1. Line a microwave safe-dish with paper towels. Spread shredded potatoes on top and microwave for 2 minutes on high. Take the pan off the heat.
2. Heat one tablespoon of oil in a nonstick skillet over medium heat.
3. Add potatoes to hot oil in batches. Use the back of a spatula to press.
4. Cook for 3 minutes on each side, or until golden brown and crispy. Repeat with the remaining potatoes, then drain on paper towels to remove any excess grease.
5. Add more oil as needed.
6. Season with salt and pepper to taste. Serve.

Nutrition: Calories: 200 kcal Protein: 4.03g Carbohydrates: 20.49g Fat: 11.73g

32. Carrot Cake Oatmeal

Preparation Time: 10 minutes
Cooking Time: 15 minutes
Servings: 1
L & G Counts : 0 leans ,0 green,2 healthy fat ,3 condiment

Ingredients:

- 1/8 cup pecans
- ½ cup finely Shredded Carrot
- 1/4 cup Old-fashioned Oats
- 5/8 cups unsweetened Nondairy Milk
- ½ tablespoon pure Maple Syrup
- ½ teaspoon ground Cinnamon
- ½ teaspoon ground Ginger
- 1/8 teaspoon ground Nutmeg
- 1 tablespoon chia seed

Directions:

1. Toast the pecans in a skillet over medium-high heat for 3–4 minutes, stirring frequently, until browned and fragrant (watch closely, as they can burn quickly).
2. Place the pecans on a cutting board and coarsely chop them. Make time for it.
3. In an 8-quart pot over medium-high heat, combine the carrot, oats, milk, maple syrup, cinnamon, ginger, and nutmeg.
4. Reduce the heat to medium-low once it begins to boil.
5. Cook for 10 minutes, stirring occasionally, uncovered.
6. Fold in the pecans and chia seeds. Serve right away.

Nutrition: Calories: 307 Fat: 17g Protein: 7g Carbohydrates: 35g Fiber: 11g

33. Chia Spinach Pancakes

Preparation Time: 10 minutes
Cooking Time: 5 minutes
Servings: 6
L & G Counts : 1 leans ,1 green,0 healthy fat ,3 condiment

Ingredients:

- 4 eggs
- ½ cup coconut flour
- 1 cup coconut milk
- ¼ cup chia seeds
- 1 cup spinach, chopped
- 1 tsp baking soda
- ½ teaspoon pepper
- ½ teaspoon salt

Directions:

1. In a mixing bowl, whisk the eggs until frothy.
2. Whisk together all of the dry ingredients before adding the egg mixture. Stir in the spinach thoroughly.
3. Melt butter in a skillet over medium heat.
4. Make the pancake with 3–4 tablespoons of batter.
5. Cook the pancake until it is lightly golden brown on both sides.
6. Plate and serve.

Nutrition: 111 Calories: 7.2g Fat: 6.3g Protein:6g

34. Feta Kale Frittata

Preparation Time: 10 minutes
Cooking Time: 30 minutes
Servings: 8
L & G Counts : 2 leans ,2 green,1 healthy fat ,2 condiment
Ingredients:

- 8 eggs, beaten
- 4 ounces feta cheese, crumbled
- 6 ounces bell pepper, roasted and diced
- 5 ounces baby kale
- 1/4 cup green onion, sliced
- 2 teaspoons olive oil

Directions:

1. In a casserole dish, heat the oil over medium-high heat.
2. Cook for 4-5 minutes, or until the kale is softened, in the Casserole.
3. Spray the slow cooker with cooking spray to prevent it from sticking.
4. Pour in the cooked kale into the slow cooker.
5. Place the green onion and bell pepper in the pot.
6. Pour the beaten eggs into the slow cooker and mix well.
7. Top with crumbled feta cheese.
8. Cook for 30 minutes on low heat.
9. Plate and serve.

Nutrition: 150 Calories: 9g Fat: 10g Protein:8g

35.Cheese Zucchini Eggplant

Preparation Time: 10 minutes
Cooking Time: 30 minutes
Servings: 8
L & G Counts : 0 leans ,2 green,1 healthy fat ,2 condiment
Ingredients:

- 1 eggplant, cut in 1-inch cubes
- 1 ½ cup spaghetti sauce
- 1 medium zucchini, cut into 1-inch pieces
- ½ cup shredded parmesan cheese

Directions:

1. Combine all of the ingredients in the crockpot and stir well.
2. Cook for 30 minutes on high, covered.
3. Mix thoroughly and serve.

Nutrition: 47 Calories: 1.2g Fat: 2.5g Protein:8g

36. Cauliflower Frittata

Preparation Time: 10 minutes
Cooking Time: 5 minutes
Servings: 1
L & G Counts : 1 leans ,0 green,1 healthy fat ,3 condiment
Ingredients:

- 1 egg
- ¼ cup cauliflower rice
- 1 tablespoon olive oil
- 1/4 teaspoon turmeric
- Pepper
- Salt

Directions:

1. Combine all ingredients except the olive oil in a mixing bowl.
2. In a frying pan, heat the oil over medium-low heat.
3. Continue to cook until the mixture is lightly browned.
4. Dish up and serve.

Nutrition: 196 Calories: 19g Fat: 7g Protein:10g

37. Vegetable Quiche

Preparation Time: 10 minutes
Cooking Time: 30 minutes
Servings: 6
L & G Counts : 2 leans ,2 green,1 healthy fat ,3 condiment
Ingredients:

- 8 eggs
- 1 cup Parmesan cheese, grated
- 1 cup unsweetened coconut milk
- 1 cup tomatoes, chopped
- 1 cup zucchini, chopped
- 1 tbsp butter
- 1/2 tsp pepper
- 1 tsp salt

Directions:

1. Preheat the oven to 400 °F. degrees Fahrenheit.
2. In a skillet over medium heat, melt the butter and cook the onion until softened.
3. Saute the tomatoes and zucchini in the pan for 4 minutes.
4. Combine eggs, cheese, milk, pepper, and salt in a mixing bowl.
5. Pour the egg mixture over the vegetables and bake for 30 minutes.
6. Cut and serve.

Nutrition: 25 Calories: 16.7g Fat: 22g Protein:15g

38. Crispy Apples

Difficulty: Easy
Preparation Time: 10 minutes
Cooking Time: 10 minutes
Servings: 4
L & G Counts : 0 leans ,0 green,1 healthy fat ,5 condiment
Ingredients:
- 5 apples
- 2 Tbsp. cinnamon powder
- 1 tablespoon maple syrup
- ½ cup water
- ¼ cup brown sugar
- ½ tablespoon nutmeg powder
- ¼ cup flour
- 4 tablespoon butter
- ¾ cup oats

Directions:
1. Take the apples in a vessel, put them in maple syrup, cinnamon, nutmeg, and water.
2. Stir in the butter, sugar, salt, flour, and oats, and then spoon a spoonful of the mixture over the apples; heat in the air fryer at 350°F for 10 minutes.
3. Serve while warm.

Nutrition: 12.4g Protein: 5.6g Fat: 387 Calories:452

39. Garlic Cauliflower Florets

Difficulty: Easy
Preparation Time: 10 minutes
Cooking Time: 20 minutes
Servings: 4
L & G Counts : - leans ,0 green,1 healthy fat ,5 condiment
Ingredients:
- 4 cups cauliflower florets
- ½ teaspoon cumin powder
- ½ teaspoon coriander powder
- 5 Garlic cloves, chopped
- 4 tablespoons olive oil
- ½ teaspoon salt

Directions:
1. Add all ingredients into the bowl and toss well.
2. Add cauliflower florets into the air fryer basket and cook at 400°F for 20 minutes. Shake halfway through.
3. Serve and enjoy.

Nutrition: Calories: 153 Fat: 14g Protein: 2.3g

40. Greek Baklava

Preparation Time: 20 minutes
Cooking Time: 20 minutes
Servings: 18
L & G Counts : 0 lean, 0 green, 1 good fat, 3 condiments
Ingredients:

- 1(16 oz.) package phyllo dough1 pound chopped nuts
- 1 cup butter
- 1 teaspoon cinnamon powder1 cup water
- 1 cup white sugar
- 1 tsp vanilla extract
- 12 cup honey

Directions:

1. Preheat the oven to 175°C or 350°F. Grease the sides and bottom of a baking dish.
2. Chop the nuts then mix with cinnamon; set it aside. Unfurl the phyllo dough, then halve the whole stack to fit the pan. Use a damp cloth to cover the phyllo to prevent drying as you proceed. Put two phyllo sheets in the pan, then butter well. Repeat to make 8 layered phyllo sheets. Scatter 2–3 tablespoons nut mixture over the sheets, then place 2 more phyllo sheets on top, butter then sprinkle with nuts. Layer as you go. The final layer should be 6 to 8 phyllo sheets deep.
3. Make square or diamond shapes with a sharp knife up to the bottom of the pan. You can slice into four long rows for diagonal shapes. Bake until crisp and golden for 50 minutes.
4. Meanwhile, boil water and sugar until the sugar melts to make the sauce; mix in honey and vanilla. Let it simmer for 20 minutes.
5. Take the baklava out of the oven, then drizzle with sauce right away; cool. Serve the baklava in cupcake papers. You can also freeze them without cover. The baklava will turn soggy when wrapped.

Nutrition: Calories: 393 Total Carbohydrate: 37.5 g Cholesterol: 27 mg Total Fat: 25.9 g Protein: 6.1 g Sodium: 196 mg

Lunch Recipes

41. Vegetable and Egg Casserole

Preparation Time: 15 minutes.
Cooking Time: 30 minutes.
Serving: 6
L & G Counts : 2 leans ,1 green,1 healthy fat ,2 condiment
Ingredients:

- 6 eggs
- 1 cup egg whites
- 1 ¼ cup cheese, shredded
- 16 ounces bag frozen spinach
- 2 cups mushrooms, sliced
- 1 bell pepper, diced

Directions:

1. At 350°F, preheat your oven.
2. Beat egg with egg whites, cheese, spinach, mushrooms, and bell pepper in a bowl.
3. Spread this egg mixture into a casserole dish.
4. Bake this casserole for 30 minutes in the oven.
5. Serve warm.

Serving Suggestion: Serve the casserole with cauliflower salad.
Variation Tip: Top the casserole with onion slices before cooking.
Nutritional Information Per Serving: Calories: 341 | Fat: 24g |Sodium: 547mg | Carbs: 36.4g | Fiber: 1.2g | Sugar: 1g | Protein: 10.3g

42. Garlic Chive Cauliflower Mash

Preparation Time: 20 minutes
Cooking Time: 18 minutes
Servings: 5
L & G Counts : 0 leans ,1 green,1 healthy fat ,4 condiment
Ingredients:

- 4 cups cauliflower
- 1/3 cup vegetarian mayonnaise
- 1 garlic clove
- ½ teaspoon kosher salt
- 1 tablespoon water
- 1/8 teaspoon pepper
- ¼ teaspoon lemon juice
- ½ teaspoon lemon zest
- 1 tablespoon Chives, minced

Directions:

1. In a bowl that is save for the microwave, add the cauliflower, mayo, garlic, water, and salt/pepper, and mix until the cauliflower is well coated. Cook on high for 15–18 minutes, until the cauliflower is almost mushy.
2. Blend the mixture in a strong blender until completely smooth, adding a little more water if the mixture is too chunky. Season with the remaining ingredients and serve.

Nutrition: Calories: 178 Total Carbohydrate: 14g Cholesterol: 18 mg Total Fat: 18 g Fiber: 4 g Protein: 2g

43. Basil Squash

Preparation Time: 5 minutes
Cooking Time: 20 minutes
Servings: 4
L & G Counts : 0 leans ,1 green,1 healthy fat ,3 condiment
Ingredients:

- 1 pound butternut squash, peeled and cut into wedges
- 2 tablespoons olive oil
- 1 tablespoon basil, chopped
- ¼ cup lemon juice
- ½ teaspoon sweet paprika
- Salt and black pepper, to taste

Directions:

1. Toss the squash with the oil, basil, and other ingredients in a pan that fits your air fryer; toss, place the pan in the air fryer, and cook at 370°F for 20 minutes.
2. Arrange on individual plates as a side dish.

Nutrition: Calories: 201, Fat: 7, Fiber: 2, Carbs: 4, Protein: 9

44. Zucchini Boat

Preparation Time: 25 minutes
Cooking Time: 20 minutes
Servings: 2
L & G Counts : 0 leans ,2 green,1 healthy fat ,5 condiment
Ingredients:

- 2 medium zucchinis
- 2 tablespoons olive oil
- ½ medium onion, diced
- 2 garlic cloves, minced
- 1 can corn, drained
- 1 cup enchilada sauce
- ½ teaspoon salt, or to taste
- ½ cup white mushrooms
- ½ cup bok Choy, chopped
- 1 teaspoon cumin
- ½ cup parmesan cheese

Directions:

1. Wash and cut the zucchini lengthwise.
2. Heat oil in a skillet and sauté onions.
3. Then, add garlic cloves and cook until aroma comes
4. Add in vegetables and cook until tender.
5. Then, add salt and enchilada sauce and cumin Mix well Turn off the heat and let it get cool
6. Scoop out the seeds of zucchinis.
7. Fill the cavity of zucchinis with the bowl mixture. Add a handful of parmesan cheese on top.
8. 4 zucchinis should be placed in the air fryer basket.
9. Set the timer for 20 minutes and the temperature to 390°F.
10. Once done, serve and enjoy.

Serving Suggestion: Serve it with ketchup
Variation Tip: None
Nutritional Information Per Serving: Calories: 472| Fat: 28.2g| Sodium: 1157mg | Carbs: 40.5g | Fiber: 10.5g | Sugar: 7.7g | Protein: 26.5g

45. Garlic Mushrooms

Preparation Time: 10 minutes
Cooking Time: 15 minutes
Servings: 3
L & G Counts : 0 leans ,1 green,1 healthy fat ,4 condiment
Ingredients:

- 10 ounces of mushrooms, washed and dried
- 1 teaspoon olive oil
- ½ teaspoon garlic powder
- 1 teaspoon Worcestershire sauce
- 1 tablespoon parsley, chopped
- Salt and black pepper, to taste
- 1 teaspoon of lemon juice

Directions:

1. Cut the washed mushrooms in half.
2. Add it to the bowl and mix in olive oil, salt, garlic powder, black pepper, Worcestershire sauce and parsley, and toss well.
3. Add mushrooms to a bowl then toss.
4. Put it into the air fryer basket and air fry at 375°F for 15 minutes.
5. Remember to toss and shake halfway through.
6. Once cooked, squeeze lemon and top with chopped parsley.

Serving Suggestion: Serve with mashed potatoes as a variation.
Variation Tip: Instead of olive oil, use vegetable oil.
Nutritional Information Per Serving: Calories: 38 | Fat: 1.9g| Sodium: 25mg | Carbs: 3.9g | Fiber: 1.1g | Sugar: 2.1g | Protein: 3.1g

46. Eggplant Ratatouille

Preparation Time: 15 minutes
Cooking Time: 15 minutes
Servings: 2
L & G Counts : 0 leans ,0 green,1 healthy fat ,3 condiment
Ingredients:

- 1 eggplant
- 1 sweet yellow pepper
- 3 cherry tomatoes
- 1/3 white onion, chopped
- ½ teaspoon garlic clove, sliced
- 1 teaspoon olive oil
- ½ teaspoon ground black pepper
- ½ teaspoon Italian seasoning

Directions:

1. Preheat the air fryer to 360°F.
2. Peel the eggplants and chop them.
3. Put the chopped eggplants in the air fryer basket.
4. Chop the cherry tomatoes and add them to the air fryer basket.
5. Then, add chopped onion, sliced garlic clove, olive oil, ground black pepper and Italian seasoning.
6. Chop the sweet yellow pepper roughly and add it to the air fryer basket.
7. Shake the vegetables gently and cook for 15 minutes.
8. Stir the meal after 8 minutes of cooking.
9. Transfer the cooked ratatouille to the serving plates.
10. Enjoy!

Nutrition: Calories: 149 Fat: 3.7g Fiber: 11.7g Carbs: 28.9g Protein: 5.1g

47. Sweet and Sour Cabbage

Preparation Time: 5 minutes
Cooking Time: 15 minutes
Servings: 2
L & G Counts : 1 leans ,2 green,1 healthy fat ,3 condiment
Ingredients:
- 5 cups shredded green cabbage
- ½ cup cooked bacon, chopped
- 3 tablespoons all-purpose flour
- 3 tablespoons brown sugar
- ¼ cup vinegar
- ½ cup water
- 1 tablespoon onion, chopped
- salt and pepper to taste

Directions:
1. Bring 5 cups of shredded cabbage to a boil for 5 minutes before draining.
2. Cook 12 cup bacon until well done, then blot with a paper towel to remove excess oil. Keep the pan drippings aside.
3. Arrange the cooked cabbage on top of the chopped bacon.
4. Combine the leftover bacon drippings, flour, and brown sugar in a mixing bowl.
5. Toss in the vinegar, water, onion, and season with salt and pepper to taste (may also use red pepper flakes).
6. Cook until thickened, then pour over cabbage and bacon. Blend until smooth.
7. Cook until thoroughly heated.
8. Serve hot..

Nutrition: Calories: 170 Protein: 17g Carbohydrate: 20g Fat: 8 g

48. Bell Pepper Bites

Preparation Time: 15 minutes.
Cooking Time: 4 minutes.
Serving: 9
L & G Counts : 0 leans ,0 green,1 healthy fat ,3 condiment
Ingredients:
- 1 medium green bell pepper
- 1 medium red bell pepper
- ¼ cup almonds, sliced
- 4 ounces low-fat cream cheese
- 1 teaspoon lemon pepper seasoning blend
- 1 teaspoon lemon juice

Directions:
1. Slice the peppers in half lengthwise.
2. Destem and deseed the peppers and cut each half into 6 more pieces.
3. Roast almonds in a skillet for 4 minutes, then grind in a food processor.
4. Mix cream cheese with lemon juice and lemon pepper in a mixing bowl for 2 minutes.
5. Stir in the almond ground and mix for 10 seconds.
6. Add this filling to the piping bag and pipe this mixture into the bell pepper piece.
7. Serve.

Serving Suggestion: Serve the peppers with chili sauce or mayo dip.
Variation Tip: Add shredded cheese to the filling.
Nutritional Information Per Serving:
Calories: 140 | Fat: 5g |Sodium: 244mg | Carbs: 16g | Fiber: 1g | Sugar: 1g | Protein: 17g

49. Strawberry and Asparagus Salad

Preparation Time: 15 minutes
Cooking Time: 5 minutes
Serving: 8
L & G Counts : 0 leans ,2 green,1 healthy fat ,3 condiment
Ingredients:

- 2 pounds (907 g) fresh asparagus, trimmed and sliced
- 3 cups fresh strawberries, hulled and sliced
- ¼ cup extra-virgin olive oil
- ¼ cup balsamic vinegar
- 2 tablespoons maple syrup
- Salt and ground black pepper, to taste

Directions:

1. Bring the asparagus to a boil in a pan with water over medium-high heat.
2. Cook the asparagus for 2 to 3 minutes, or until it is al dente.
3. Immediately drain the asparagus and place it in a bowl of ice water to cool completely.
4. Pat the asparagus dry with paper towels.
5. Combine the asparagus and strawberries in a large mixing bowl.
6. In a small mixing bowl, combine the olive oil, vinegar, honey, salt, and black pepper.
7. Gently toss the asparagus-strawberry mixture with the dressing to coat. 1 hour before serving, place in the refrigerator.

Nutrition: Calories: 88 Protein: 3.04g Carbohydrate: 13.79g Fat: 3.21 g

50. Pea Salad

Preparation Time: 10 minutes
Cooking Time: 15 minutes
Servings: 1
L & G Counts : 0 leans ,2 green,1 healthy fat ,3 condiment
Ingredients:

- 1/2 cup chickpeas, rinsed and drained
- 1/2 cups peas, divided
- Salt, to taste
- 1 tablespoon olive oil
- ½ cup buttermilk
- Pepper, to taste
- 2 cups pea greens
- ½ carrots shaved
- ¼ cup snow peas, trimmed

Directions:

1. Add the chickpeas and half of the peas to your food processor.
2. Season with salt.
3. Pulse until smooth. Set aside.
4. In a bowl, toss the remaining peas in oil, milk, salt and pepper.
5. Transfer the mixture to your food processor.
6. Process until pureed.
7. Transfer this mixture to a bowl.
8. Arrange the pea greens on a serving plate.
9. Top with the shaved carrots and snow peas.
10. Stir in the pea and milk dressing.
11. Serve with the reserved chickpea hummus.

Nutrition: Calories:214 Fat: 8.6 g Carbohydrates 27.3 g Protein: 8 g

Dinner Recipes

51. Chives Beets Mix

Preparation Time: 10 minutes
Cooking Time: 25 minutes
Servings: 4
L & G Counts : 0 leans ,1 green,1 healthy fat ,3 condiment
Ingredients:

- 4 beets, peeled and cut into wedges
- 2 tablespoons olive oil
- 1 tablespoon chives, chopped
- 2 garlic cloves, minced
- Salt and black pepper, to taste
- 1 teaspoon cumin, ground

Directions:

1. In your air fryer's basket, combine the beets with the oil and the other ingredients, toss and cook at 380°F for 25 minutes.
2. Divide the mix between plates and serve.

Nutrition: Calories: 100, Fat: 2, Fiber: 4, Carbohydrates 7, Protein: 5g

52. Green Pea Guacamole

Preparation Time: 15 minutes
Cooking Time: 30 minutes
Servings: 4
L & G Counts : 0 leans ,1 green,0 healthy fat ,3 condiment
Ingredients:

- 1 teaspoon crushed garlic
- 1 chopped tomato
- 3 cups frozen green peas (chopped)
- 5 green chopped onions
- 1/6 teaspoon hot sauce
- ½ teaspoon grounded cumin
- ½ cup lime juice

Directions:

1. Blend the peas, garlic, lime juice and cumin until it is smoothened.
2. Stir in the tomatoes, green onion and hot sauce into the mixture.
3. Season with salt to taste.
4. Place it in the refrigerator for at least 25 minutes, covered. This allows the flavor to blend well.

Nutrition: Calories: 40.7 Fat: 0.2 g Cholesterol: 0.0 mg Sodium: 157.4 mg Carbohydrates: 7.6 g Dietary Fiber: 1.7 g Protein: 2.7 g

53. Spicy Red Cabbage

Preparation Time: 10 minutes
Cooking Time: 15 minutes
Servings: 4
L & G Counts : 0 leans ,0 green,1 healthy fat ,4 condiment
Ingredients:

- 6 cups red cabbage, shredded
- ½ cup yellow onion, chopped
- 1 tablespoon olive oil
- 1 teaspoon hot paprika
- Salt and black pepper, to taste
- 1 tablespoon apple cider vinegar

Directions:

1. Set your instant pot in Stir-fry mode, add oil, heat; add onion, stir, and sauté for 5 minutes
2. Stir in the remaining ingredients; cover and cook for 10 minutes on high heat. Allow for 10 minutes of natural pressure before dividing the mixture between dishes and serving as a garnish.

Nutrition: Calories: 132 Fat: seven Fiber: 3 Carbs: 6 Protein: 8

54. Family Favorite Stuffed Mushrooms

Preparation Time: 4 minutes
Cooking Time: 12 minutes
Servings: 2
L & G Counts : 0 leans ,0 green,1 healthy fat ,5 condiment
Ingredients:

- 2 teaspoons cumin powder
- 4 garlic cloves, peeled and minced
- 1 small onion, peeled and chopped
- 18 medium-sized white mushrooms
- Fine sea salt and freshly ground black pepper, to your liking
- A pinch ground allspice
- 2 tablespoons olive oil

Directions:

1. First, clean the mushrooms; remove the middle stalks from the mushrooms to prepare the "shells."
2. Grab a mixing dish and thoroughly combine the remaining ingredients. Fill the mushrooms with the prepared mixture.
3. Cook the mushrooms at 345°F heat for 12 minutes. Enjoy!

Nutrition: Calories: 179 Fat: 14.7g Carbs: 8.5g Protein: 5.5g Sugar: 4.6g Fiber: 2.6g

55. Arugula Lentil Salad

Preparation Time: 5 minutes
Cooking Time: 7 minutes
Servings: 2
L & G Counts : 0 leans ,2 green,1 healthy fat ,3 condiment
Level of Difficulty: Easy
Ingredients:

- 1-2 tablespoons balsamic vinegar
- ¾ cups cashews
- 1 handful arugula/rocket
- 1 cup brown lentils, cooked
- 3 Slices bread, whole wheat
- 5-6 sun-dried tomatoes in oil
- 1 chili / jalapeño
- 1 tablespoon olive oil
- 1 onion
- Salt and pepper, to taste

Optional:

- 1 tablespoon honey
- 1 small handful raisins

Directions:

1. Toast the cashews in a pan over low heat for about 3 to 4 minutes. Then, dump them into a pot of salad. Dice and fry the onion in one-third of the olive oil over low heat for around 3 minutes.
2. In the meantime, cut your chili/jalapeño and dried tomatoes. In the grill, add them and fry for the next 1–2 minutes.
3. Slice the bread into large croutons. Shift the mixture of onions into a large container. Put the rest of the oil in your pan and cook the sliced bread until it's crispy seasoning with salt and pepper.
4. Now, clean the arugula and put it in the bowl. Bring in the lentils, too, and blend everything over. Use salt, pepper and balsamic vinegar to season. With the croutons, eat. Super delicious!

Nutrition: Calories:270 Carbs:27g Fat: 15g Protein: 12g

56. Peanut Soup

Preparation Time: 15 minutes
Cooking Time: 10 minutes
Servings: 3
L & G Counts : 0 leans ,2 green,1 healthy fat ,4 condiment
Level of Difficulty: Easy
Ingredients:

- 1 cup brown rice (uncooked)
- A few dashes hot sauce
- 1 tablespoon soy sauce
- 1 clove garlic
- 1 small carrot
- 1 tablespoon tomato paste
- Handful peanuts
- 3-4 tablespoon peanut butter
- ½ medium courgette (zucchini)
- ½ red onion
- 700 ml vegetable broth
- 1 ginger, fresh or ½ Tbsp. powdered ginger

Directions:

1. Prepare the brown rice. Put to the boil 700ml of vegetable broth. Split the cabbage, carrot and courgette, and add them to the broth. Garlic and ginger are also added to the broth.
2. Put in the peanuts. Add some peanut butter and tomato paste to your mixture. Add some soy sauce last, but ensure it's not still too salty. Let the rice boil until it is done. Serve in a pot, eat it instantly.

Nutrition: Calories: 130 Carbs: 13g Fat: 7g Protein: 4g

57. Sweet Potato Soup

Preparation Time: 10 minutes
Cooking Time: 20 minutes
Servings: 4
L & G Counts : 0 leans ,0 green,2 healthy fat ,7 condiment
Level of Difficulty: Normal
Ingredients:

- 2 tablespoons olive oil
- 1 medium onion
- 1 Bell pepper, red
- 2 cloves garlic
- 1 tablespoon cinnamon
- 1 ginger, fresh, or 1 Tbsp. dried ginger
- 2 cups vegetable broth
- 1 tablespoon peanut butter
- ½ tablespoon cayenne pepper
- ½ cup tomato puree
-

- 2 ½ cups large sweet potato, chopped
- 1 tablespoon soy sauce (low sodium if necessary)
- Salt and pepper, to taste
- 1 tablespoon vinegar or lemon juice
- 2 tablespoons maple syrup
- Peanuts (to garnish)
- ½ lime (juiced)
- ¼ cup cilantro/coriander, fresh

Directions:
1. Cut the onions and dump them into the oil in a pot on low to moderate heat. For around 5 minutes, let the onion cook steadily; it should begin to turn transparent.
2. Sweet potatoes should be peeled and sliced into chunks. Cut the garlic, bell pepper, and ginger, and put them into the bowl. Add them now if you're using dried herbs.
3. Also, put in cinnamon and cayenne pepper. Cook and add the soy sauce, peanut butter, vinegar, and tomato for the next 2 minutes. Stir well and apply a shot of broth.
4. Add the sweet potatoes and the majority of the broth and bring to a boil over medium heat. Add them now if you are using raw herbs. Stir regularly and after 10–15 minutes, confirm the sweet potatoes are cooked.
5. Season using salt and pepper, maple syrup and lime juice, and allow another swirl. If you used a cinnamon stick, then throw it out now.
6. Use a hand liquidizer or offer the soup a blend on a blender if you do not have one. Garnish with peanuts, then serve with a side if desired — fresh bread is an obvious option!

Nutrition: Calories: 110 Carbs: 23g Fat: 1g Protein: 2g

58. Baba Ganoush

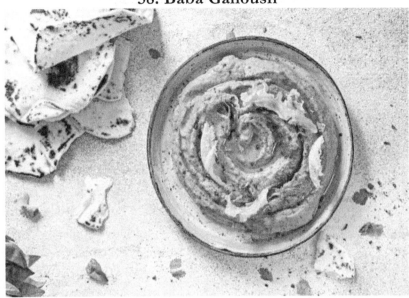

Preparation Time: 15 minutes
Cooking Time: 0 minutes
Servings: 8-10
L & G Counts : 0 leans ,0 green,1 healthy fat ,3 condiment
Level of Difficulty: Normal
Ingredients:

- 3 small eggplants
- Salt and pepper, to taste
- 1 tablespoon paprika
- 1 tablespoon olive oil (plus a splash when serving the dish)
- 1 lemon (juiced)
- 1 tablespoon tahini (or sesame paste is fine too)
- 1 cloves garlic

Optional:

- 1 tablespoon cilantro/coriander, fresh
- Handful pomegranate seeds

Directions:

1. Warm your oven to 180°C. Place the eggplants on an oven tray with a drizzle of olive oil and some spices. Prick mini holes in it using a toothpick.
2. Put the cloves of garlic; no reason for them to peel. Roast before tender for about 25–30 minutes.
3. Let it cool, then slice them open and slice out the flesh. Using a beater or food blender, mix the eggplant flesh with the juice of the lemon.
4. Put in a bowl with some paprika and a dash of olive oil for garnish. You can serve as a dip with pitas, flatbread, or nachos, or as a side dish with the main dish.
5. For optional, stir in the pomegranate seeds and cilantro to add an extra kick of freshness to this lovely Baba Ganoush.

Nutrition: Calories: 349 Carbs: 5g Fat: 29g Protein: 12g

59. Colorful Tabbouleh Salad

Preparation Time: 15 minutes
Cooking Time: 0 minutes
Servings: 4
L & G Counts : 0 leans ,2 green,1 healthy fat ,3 condiment
Level of Difficulty: Normal
Ingredients:

- 1 cup instant couscous - Salt and pepper, to taste
- 4 tablespoon olive oil
- 2 ½ tablespoon tomato paste
- 2 small tomato
- 7 sun-dried tomatoes in oil
- 2 spring onions
- 1 bunch parsley, fresh
- ½ cucumber - 1 carrot
- 1 lemon (juiced)
- 1 ½ cups vegetable broth (or just use water)

Optional:

- 1 tablespoon Tabasco (or similar chili sauce)
- 2 tablespoons pumpkin seeds (or roasted sunflower seeds, to use as garnish)
- ½ bunch mint, fresh

Directions:

1. Using vegetable broth for the tastiest results, cook the couscous according to packet instructions. Now, add hot vegetable broth to it until it is all filled with couscous.
2. Position a tea towel over the end. Give it a slight swirl after 3–4 minutes to make it fluffy. For 1 more minute, cover again. 3. Rub the carrots and dice the cucumber, peppers, tomatoes (fresh and sun-dried), mint, and parsley in the meantime. 4. With the cooked couscous, add the lemon juice, tomato paste, olive oil, salt, pepper, Tabasco sauce and chopped and grated vegetables and herbs. Mix and serve. If using, garnish with seeds.

Nutrition: Calories: 80 Carbs: 6g Fat: 5g Protein: 1g

60. Easy Cauliflower Curry

Preparation Time: 10 minutes
Cooking Time: 20 minutes
Servings: 4
L & G Counts : 0 leans ,2 green,1 healthy fat ,5 condiment
Level of Difficulty: Normal
Ingredients:

- 1 bunch cilantro/coriander, fresh
- 1 tablespoon maple syrup
- 1 tablespoon curry powder
- 1 lime (juiced)
- 1 can coconut milk
- ½ tablespoon curry paste
- 1 tablespoon olive oil
-
- 2 thumbs ginger, fresh
- 1 cup green beans
- 1 small-medium potato
- ½ red peppers
- 2 large Onions
- Salt
- ½ medium tomato

Directions:

1. Cut the cauliflower into bite-sized bits; slice the potatoes and bell pepper into small pieces. The tips of the green beans are separated and sliced in two.
2. Dice the onion and slice the ginger finely. Add some oil to a pan and add the ginger over medium heat.
3. Add the onion and bell pepper as soon as it begins to release its scent (about 2 minutes) and sauté (fry over medium heat) for 5 minutes. Mix in the paste of the curry, stir and simmer for another 2 minutes.
4. To dissolve the curry paste, stir in a little coconut milk, and then add the remainder. Set to high heat before the milk begins to boil.
5. Reduce to low heat and apply lime juice, curry powder, salt, and maple syrup until boiling. Only mix well.
6. Now it is time for the potatoes and cauliflower to be added. Simmer for 5 minutes, add the green beans and leave to simmer for another 5 minutes.
7. Give a taste test to the curry, see if you need any more salt, sugar, or lime to apply. You can even add a little more curry paste as well. It's ready to serve until you're comfortable.
8. Serve on top of sliced new cilantro. With this lovely curry meal, rice or quinoa goes well!

Nutrition: Calories: 475 Carbs: 45g Fat: 24g Protein: 26g

VEGANS

Breakfast Recipes

61. Oat Porridge with Cherry & Coconut

Preparation Time: 10 minutes
Cooking Time: 0 minutes
Servings: 3
L & G Counts : 0 leans ,0 green,1 healthy fat ,3 condiment
Ingredients:

- 1 ½ cup regular oats
- 3 cups coconut milk
- 4 tablespoons Chia seed
- 3 tablespoons Raw cacaos
- Coconut shavings
- Dark chocolate shavings
- Fresh or frozen tart cherries
- A pinch stevia, optional
- Maple syrup, to taste (optional)

Directions:

1. In a medium saucepan over medium heat, bring the oats, milk, stevia, and cacao to a boil. Reduce the heat to low and cook the oats until they are cooked to your satisfaction.
2. Drizzle maple syrup over the porridge and top with dark chocolate, chia seeds, and coconut shavings.

Nutrition: Calories: 343 kcal Protein: 15.64g Carbohydrates: 41.63g Fat: 12.78g

62. Vegan-Friendly Banana Bread

Preparation Time: 15 minutes
Cooking Time: 30 minutes
Servings: 4-6
L & G Counts : 0 leans ,0 green,1 healthy fat ,5 condiment
Ingredients:

- 2 Ripe bananas, mashed
- 1/3 cup brewed coffee
- 3 tablespoons chia seeds
- 6 tablespoons water
- ½ cup soft vegan butter
- ½ cup maple syrup
- 2 cups flour
- 2 tablespoons Baking powder
- 1 tablespoons Cinnamon powder

Directions:

1. Preheat the oven to 350°F.
2. In a small bowl, combine the chia seeds and 6 tablespoons of water. After thoroughly mixing, set aside.
3. In a mixing bowl, combine the vegan butter and maple syrup with a hand mixer until fluffy. Combine the chia seeds and the mashed bananas in a mixing bowl.
4. Combine thoroughly, then add the coffee.
5. In the meantime, sift together all of the dry ingredients (flour, baking powder, cinnamon powder) and gradually add to the wet.
6. Combine all of the ingredients and pour into a baking pan lined with parchment paper.
7. Bake for about 30 minutes, or until a toothpick inserted into the bread comes out clean.
8. Allow the bread to cool before serving.

Nutrition: Calories: 371 kcal Protein: 5.59g Fat: 16.81g Carbohydrates: 49.98g

63. Healthy Waffles

Preparation Time: 10 minutes
Cooking Time: 10 minutes
Servings: 4
L & G Counts : 0 leans ,0 green,1 healthy fat ,3 condiment
Ingredients:

- 8 drops liquid stevia
- ½ teaspoon baking soda
- 1 tablespoon chia seeds
- ¼ cup water
- 2 tablespoons sunflower seed butter
- 1 teaspoon cinnamon
- 1 avocado, peel, pitted, and mashed
- 1 teaspoon vanilla
- 1 tablespoon lemon juice
- 3 tablespoons coconut flour

Directions:

1. Preheat the waffle maker.
2. Soak chia seeds in water for 5 minutes in a small bowl.
3. In a mixing bowl, combine sunflower seed butter, lemon juice, vanilla, stevia, chia mixture, and avocado.
4. In a mixing bowl, combine cinnamon, baking soda, and coconut flour.
5. Combine the wet and dry ingredients thoroughly.
6. Pour the waffle batter into the hot waffle iron and cook for 3–5 minutes on each side.
7. Plate and serve.

Nutrition: 220 Calories: 17g Fat: 5.1g Protein:8g

64. Chia Pudding

Preparation Time: 20 minutes
Cooking Time: 0 minutes
Servings: 2
L & G Counts : 0 leans ,0 green,1 healthy fat ,1 condiment
Ingredients:

- 4 tablespoon chia seeds
- 1 cup unsweetened coconut milk
- ½ cup raspberries

Directions:

1. Add raspberry and coconut milk into a blender and blend until smooth.
2. Pour the mixture into a glass jar.
3. Add chia seeds in a jar and stir well.
4. Place the jar in the refrigerator for 3 hours after sealing it with a lid.
5. Serve chilled and enjoy.

Nutrition: Calories: 360 Fat: 33 g Carbs: 13 g Sugar: 5 g Protein: 6 g Cholesterol: 0 mg

65. Cinnamon Coconut Porridge

Preparation Time: 5 minutes
Cooking Time: 0 minutes
Servings: 1
L & G Counts : 0 leans ,0 green,3 healthy fat ,2 condiment
Ingredients:

- 2 tablespoons shredded coconut
- 1 tablespoon ground flax seeds
- 2 tablespoons hemp hearts
- ⅛ teaspoon cinnamon
- ⅛ teaspoon stevia powder
- ½ cup boiling water
- Fresh mixed berries, to top

Directions:

1. Add all ingredients except for fresh mixed berries and water to a serving bowl and stir to combine.
2. Add boiling water. Stir.
3. Allow the porridge to sit until it reaches a suitable eating temperature.
4. As it cools, the porridge will thicken.
5. Top with fresh mixed berries and serve.

Nutrition: Total Fat: 31.5g Cholesterol: 0mg Sodium: 8mg Total Carbohydrates: 9.8g Dietary fiber: 9g Protein: 21.7g Calcium: 49mg Potassium: 95mg Iron: 11mg Vitamin D: 0mcg

66. Vanilla Shake

Preparation Time: 5 minutes
Cooking Time: 0 minutes
Servings: 1
L & G Counts : 0 leans ,0 green,1 healthy fat ,2 condiment
Ingredients:

- ½ cup water
- 1 teaspoon Vanilla Shake Fueling
- ½ cup unsweetened almond milk
- 1 teaspoon Gingerbread Fueling
- 8 ice cubes

Directions:

1. Take a blender, place all ingredients, and pulse until smooth.
2. Pour in serving glasses and serve.

Serving Suggestions: Garnish it with whipped cream and sprinkle chocolate over it.
Variation Tip: You can also make a thick milkshake with ice cream.
Nutrition per Serving: Calories: 130 | Fat: 3.3g|Sat Fat: 0.2g|Carbohydrates: 15g|Fiber: 4.5g|Sugar: 6g|Protein: 13g

67. Pumpkin Waffles

Preparation Time: 10 minutes
Cooking Time: 8 minutes
Servings: 4
L & G Counts : 0 leans ,0 green,1 healthy fat ,3 condiment
Ingredients:

- ½ cup water
- 4 tablespoons sugar-free pancake syrup
- Pinch ground cinnamon
- ½ teaspoon pumpkin pie spice
- 2 tablespoons 100% canned pumpkin
- 4 teaspoons Golden Pancake

Directions:

1. Heat a mini waffle iron so grease it.
2. In a bowl, add all ingredients apart from flapjack sweetener and blend till well integrated.
3. Place half the mixture into the preheated waffle iron and cook for 3–4 minutes or till golden brown.
4. Repeat with the remaining mixture.
5. Serve warm and enjoy!

Serving Suggestions: Serve with butter, syrup, and pumpkin seeds.
Variation Tip: You can also use honey instead of syrup.
Nutrition per Serving: Calories: 148 | Fat: 3.1g|Sat Fat: 0.3g|Carbohydrates: 7.5g|Fiber: 3.2g|Sugar: 11.4g|Protein: 3.6g

68. Brownie Pudding cups

Preparation Time: 10 minutes
Cooking Time: 1 minute
Servings: 2
L & G Counts : 0 leans ,0 green,1 healthy fat ,2 condiment
Ingredients:

- 2 teaspoons Chocolate Pudding Mix
- 2 tablespoons sugar-free caramel syrup
- 1 cup water, divided
- 2 teaspoons Brownie Mix

Directions:

1. In a bowl, add the Pudding Mix and 3 tablespoons of water, and mix well.
2. Divide the mixture equally and microwave for a minute.
3. Take it out from the microwave and chill it down completely.
4. In a bowl, add the Pudding combine and remaining water, and mix well.
5. Place the pudding mixture over the brownie mixture equally.
6. Drizzle with caramel sweetening and with a knife swirl caramel into pudding.
7. Refrigerate until set completely before serving.

Serving Suggestions: Top with chocolate syrup before serving.
Variation Tip: you can also use caramel syrup for a taste.
Nutrition per Serving: Calories: 106 | Fat: 2.1g | Sat Fat: 0.4g | Carbohydrates: 21.8g | Fiber: 0.5g | Sugar: 0g | Protein: 0.6g

69. Papaya Acai Bowl

Preparation Time: 25 minutes
Cooking Time: 0 minutes
Servings: 4
L & G Counts : 0 leans ,0 green,1 healthy fat ,3 condiment
Ingredients:

- 1 banana
- 1 cup blueberries
- 1 cup coconut milk
- ¼ cup water
- 2 tablespoons hemp seeds
- 2 tablespoons honey
- 1 papaya, peeled and cubed
- ¼ cup sliced almonds

Directions:

1. Combine the banana, blueberries, coconut milk, water, hemp seeds, and honey in a blender, and pulse until smooth.
2. Pour the mixture into bowls and top with papaya and sliced almonds.
3. Serve right away.

Nutrition per serving: Calories: 306 Fat: 19.4g Protein: 4.9g Carbohydrates: 34g

70. Honey Oatmeal Pudding

Preparation Time: 10 minutes
Cooking Time: 20 minutes
Servings: 4
L & G Counts : 0 leans ,0 green,1 healthy fat ,3 condiment
Ingredients:

- 1 cup water
- 1 cup coconut milk
- 1 cup rolled oats
- ¼ cup raw honey
- ½ teaspoon vanilla extract
- 1 pinch ground ginger
- 2 tablespoons ground flaxseeds

Directions:

1. Combine all the ingredients in a saucepan and place over low heat.
2. Cook for 10 minutes, stirring all the time until the pudding is thickened.
3. Serve the pudding warm.

Nutrition per serving: Calories: 300 Fat: 16.7g Protein: 4.8g Carbohydrates: 35.7g

Lunch Recipes

71. Spiced Couscous

Preparation Time: 10 minutes
Cooking Time: 15 minutes
Servings: 6
L & G Counts : 0 leans ,0 green,0 healthy fat , 7 condiment
Ingredients:

- 2 tablespoons extra-virgin olive oil
- ½ onion, minced
- 1 orange juice
- 1 orange zest
- ½ teaspoon garlic powder
- ½ teaspoon ground cumin
- ½ teaspoon sea salt
- ¼ teaspoon ground ginger
- ¼ teaspoon ground all spice
- ¼ teaspoon ground cinnamon
- 1/8 teaspoon freshly ground black pepper
- 2 cups water
- 1 cup whole-wheat couscous
- ¼ cup dried apricots, chopped
- ¼ cup dried cranberries

Directions:

1. In a medium saucepan over medium-high heat, heat the olive oil until it shimmers.
2. Cook, stirring occasionally, for about 3 minutes, or until the onion is soft.
3. Combine the orange juice and zest, garlic powder, cumin, sea salt, ginger, all spice, cinnamon, pepper, and water in a mixing bowl. Bring the water to a boil.
4. Combine the couscous, apricots, and cranberries in a mixing bowl. Remove from the heat and cover the pot with a lid. Set aside for 5 minutes, covered. Fluff the rice with a fork.

Nutrition: Calories: 181 Fat: 6 g Saturated Fat: 1 g Carbs: 30 g Fiber: 4 g Protein: 6 g Sugar: 5 g Cholesterol: 0 mg Sodium: 157 mg

72. Delicious Ratatouille

Preparation Time: 10 minutes
Cooking Time: 15 minutes
Servings: 6
L & G Counts : 0 leans ,0 green,1 healthy fat ,3 condiment
Ingredients:

- 1 eggplant, diced)
- 3 garlic cloves, chopped
- 1 onion, diced
- 3 tomatoes, diced
- 2 bell peppers, diced
- 1 tablespoon vinegar
- 1 ½ tablespoon olive oil
- 2 tablespoons herb de Provence
- Pepper
- Salt

Directions:

1. Preheat the air fryer to 400°F.
2. Add all ingredients into the bowl and toss well.
3. Add vegetable mixture into the air fryer basket and cook for 15 minutes. Stir halfway through.
4. Serve and enjoy.

Nutrition: 83 Calories: 4g Fat: 2g Protein:

73. Healthy Asparagus Spears

Preparation Time: 10 minutes
Cooking Time: 15 minutes
Servings: 4
L & G Counts : 0 leans ,2 green,1 healthy fat ,3 condiment
Ingredients:

- 35 asparagus spears, cut the
- ½ teaspoon garlic powder
- 1 tablespoon olive oil
- Pepper
- Salt
- ¼ teaspoon onion powder

Directions:

1. Place the asparagus in a large mixing bowl. Drizzle with olive oil.
2. Season with onion powder, garlic powder, pepper, and salt to taste. Toss gently.
3. Place the asparagus in the air fryer basket and cook for 15 minutes at 375°F.
4. Plate and serve.

Nutrition: 75 Calories: 4g Fat: 4g Protein:

74. Spicy Brussels Sprouts

Preparation Time: 10 minutes
Cooking Time: 14 minutes
Servings: 2
L & G Counts : 0 leans ,1 green,1 healthy fat ,3 condiment
Ingredients:

- ½ pound Brussels sprouts, trimmed and halved
- ½ teaspoon chili powder
- ¼ teaspoon cayenne
- ½ tablespoon olive oil
- ¼ teaspoon smoked paprika

Directions:

1. Mix all ingredients into the large bowl and toss well.
2. Place the Brussels sprouts in the air fryer basket and cook for 14 minutes at 370°F.
3. Plate and serve.

Nutrition: 82 Calories: 4g Fat: 4g Protein:

75. Air Fryer Bell Peppers

Preparatin Time: 10 minutes
Cooking Time: 8 minutes
Servings: 3
L & G Counts : 0 leans ,0 green,1 healthy fat ,0 condiment
Ingredients:

- ¼ teaspoon onion powder
- 3 cups bell peppers, cut into pieces
- 1 teaspoon olive oil
- 1/4 teaspoon garlic powder

Directions:

1. Mix all ingredients into the large bowl and toss well.
2. Transfer bell peppers into the air fryer basket and cook at 360°F for 8 minutes. Stir halfway through.
3. Serve and enjoy.

Nutrition: 52 Calories: 2g Fat: 1.2g Protein:

76. Air Fried Tasty Eggplant

Preparation Time: 10 minutes
Cooking Time: 12 minutes
Servings: 2
L & G Counts : 0 leans ,0 green,1 healthy fat ,3 condiment
Ingredients:

- 1 eggplant, cut into cubes
- ¼ teaspoon oregano
- 1 tablespoon olive oil
- ½ teaspoon garlic powder
- ¼ teaspoon chili powder

Directions:

1. Incorporate all ingredients into the huge bowl and toss well.
2. Transfer eggplant into the air fryer basket and cook at 390°F for 12 minutes. Stir halfway through.
3. Serve and enjoy.

Nutrition: 120 Calories: 7g Fat: 2g Protein:

77. Air Fryer Broccoli & Brussels Sprouts

Preparation Time: 10 minutes
Cooking Time: 30 minutes
Servings: 6
L & G Counts : 0 leans ,1 green,1 healthy fat ,4 condiment
Ingredients:

- 1 pound Brussels sprouts, cut ends
- 1 pound broccoli, cut into florets
- 1 teaspoon paprika
- 1 teaspoon garlic powder
- ½ teaspoon pepper
- 3 tablespoon olive oil
- ¾ teaspoon salt

Directions:

1. Toss together all of the ingredients in a large mixing bowl.
2. Place the vegetable mixture in the air fryer basket and cook for 30 minutes at 370°F.
3. Plate and serve.

Nutrition: 125 Calories: 7.6g Fat: 5g Protein:

78. Asian Stir Fry

Preparation Time: 15 minutes
Cooking Time: 10 minutes
Servings: 4
L & G Counts : 0 leans ,2 green,1 healthy fat ,3 condiment

Ingredients:

- 1 teaspoon Olive oil
- 1 teaspoon Low Soy Sodium: Sauce
- 1 Lime Wedge (1/8 Lime)
- ¾ cup Broccoli blossoms
- ½ cup Sliced Chestnuts
- ¼ hp. Red bell pepper split
- ¼ hp. Freshwater
- New ground potatoes, to taste

Directions:

1. Prepare veggies.
2. Add oil, soy sauce, and lime wedge juice in a medium to a large skillet, and put on medium heat.
3. Add water to the saucepan and stir until the water gets warm.
4. Next, add the vegetables and thoroughly mix to ensure that they are all consumed.
5. Cook, covered, over medium-high to high heat until the vegetables are tender and the liquid has completely evaporated.

Nutrition: 13g Carbohydrates 4g Protein: 8g Fat:

79. Turmeric Roasted Cauliflower Bites

Preparation Time: 10 minutes
Cooking Time: 35 minutes
Servings: 4
L & G Counts : 0 leans ,0 green,1 healthy fat ,4 condiment

Ingredients:

- 1 ½ heads cauliflower, cut into florets
- 4 teaspoons canola oil
- ½ teaspoon turmeric
- ½ teaspoon cayenne
- 1 lemon, juiced
- 1 ½ teaspoon curry powder
- 2 garlic cloves, minced
- ½ teaspoon each salt and ground black pepper

Directions:

1. Preheat the oven to 450 degrees Fahrenheit.
2. Combine all of the ingredients in a large zip-lock bag. Toss until everything is well combined.
3. Arrange the cauliflower in a single layer on a baking sheet lined with foil. Roast for 30–35 minutes, stirring occasionally, until tender and golden brown.
4. Plate and enjoy!

Nutrition: Calories: 78; Net carbs: 3g; Fiber: 2g; Protein: 2.5g; Fat: 4.9g

80. Spinach Lentil Stew

Preparation Time: 13 minutes
Cooking Time: 27 minutes
Servings: 8
L & G Counts : 0 leans ,2 green,1 healthy fat ,7 condiment
Ingredients:

- 3 tablespoons extra-virgin olive oil
- 2 garlic cloves, chopped
- 2 shallots, sliced
- 1 red bell pepper, cored and diced
- 1 carrot, diced
- 1 celery stalk, diced
- ½ teaspoon turmeric powder
- ¼ teaspoon chili powder
- ½ teaspoon garam masala
- 1 cup diced tomatoes
- 1 cup green lentils, rinsed
- 2 cups water
- 1 bay leaf
- Salt and pepper, to taste
- 2 cups baby spinach

Directions:

1. In a saucepan, heat the oil. Cook for 2 minutes, or until the garlic and shallots are softened.
2. Season with salt and pepper and add the remaining ingredients, except the spinach.
3. Cook for 20 minutes on low heat, or until creamy and cooked through.
4. Cook for 5 minutes more after adding the spinach.
5. Serve the stew hot and hot.

Nutrition per serving: Calories: 147 Fat: 5.6g Protein: 7.0g Carbohydrates: 18.1g

Dinner Recipes

81. Sesame Broccoli Mix

Preparation Time: 5 minutes
Cooking Time: 14 minutes
Servings: 4
L & G Counts : 0 leans ,2 green,1 healthy fat ,3 condiment
Ingredients:

- 1 pound broccoli florets
- 1 tablespoon sesame oil
- 1 teaspoon sesame seeds, toasted
- 1 red onion, sliced
- 1 tablespoon lime juice
- 1 teaspoon chili powder
- Salt and black pepper, to taste

Directions:

1. In your air fryer, combine the broccoli with the oil, sesame seeds and the other ingredients, toss and cook at 380°F for 14 minutes.
2. Divide between plates and serve.

Nutrition: Calories: 141, Fat: 3, Fiber: 4, Carbohydrates 4, Protein: 2

82. Bell-Pepper Wrapped in Tortilla

Preparation Time: 5 minutes
Cooking Time: 15 minutes
Servings: 1
L & G Counts : 0 leans ,0 green,1 healthy fat ,3 condiment
Ingredients:

- ¼ small red bell pepper, chopped
- ¼ small yellow onion, diced
- ¼ tablespoon water
- ½ cobs grilled corn kernels
- 1 large tortilla
- 1 piece commercial vegan nuggets, chopped
- Mixed greens for garnish

Directions:

1. Preheat the Instant Crisp Air Fryer to 400° degrees Fahrenheit.
2. Sauté the vegan nuggets, onions, bell peppers, and corn kernels in a skillet over medium heat. Place aside.
3. Place filling inside the corn tortillas.
4. Close the lid of the air fryer. Fold the tortillas and place them in the Instant Crisp Air Fryer for 15 minutes, or until crispy.
5. Garnish with mixed greens.

Nutrition: Calories: 548 Fat: 20.7g Protein: 46g

83. Fennel and Arugula Salad with Fig Vinaigrette

Preparation Time: 15 minutes
Cooking Time: 10 minutes
Servings: 6
L & G Counts : 0 leans ,1 green,1 healthy fat ,3 condiment
Ingredients:

- 5 ounces washed and dried arugula
- 1 small fennel bulb, it can be either shaved or tiny sliced
- 2 tablespoons extra-virgin oil or any cooking oil
- 1 teaspoon lemon zest
- ½ teaspoon salt
- Pepper (freshly ground)
- Pecorino

Directions:

1. In a serving bowl, combine the arugula and shaved fennel.
2. On another bowl, mix the olive oil or cooking oil, lemon zest, salt, and pepper
3. Shake together until it becomes creamy and smooth.
4. Pour and dress over the salad, tossing gently for it to combine.
5. Peel or shave out some slices of pecorino and put them on top of the salad.
6. Serve immediately.

Nutrition: Protein: 2.1 g Carbohydrates: 14.3 g Dietary Fiber: 3.4 g Sugar: 9.1 g Fat: 9.7 g

84. Bell Pepper-Corn Wrapped in Tortilla

Preparation Time: 5 minutes
Cooking Time: 15 minutes
Servings: 4
L & G Counts : 0 leans ,1 green,1 healthy fat ,3 condiment
Ingredients:

- 1 small red bell pepper, chopped
- 1 small yellow onion, diced
- 1 tablespoon water
- 2 grilled corn kernels
- 4 large tortillas
- 4 pieces commercial vegan nuggets, chopped

Directions:

1. Preheat the air fryer to 400 degrees Fahrenheit.
2. Sauté the vegan nuggets with the onions, bell peppers, and corn kernels in a skillet over medium heat.Place aside.
3. Stuff the corn tortillas with the filling.
4. Place the tortillas in the air fryer and cook for 15 minutes, or until the tortilla wraps are crispy.
5. Serve with mixed greens on top.

Nutrition: Calories: 548 Carbohydrates: 43.54g Protein: 46.73g Fat: 20.76g

85. Black Bean Burger with Garlic-Chipotle

Preparation Time: 10 minutes
Cooking Time: 20 minutes
Servings: 3
L & G Counts : 0 leans ,0 green,1 healthy fat ,5 condiment
Ingredients:

- ½ cup corn kernels
- ½ teaspoon chipotle powder
- ½ teaspoon garlic powder
- ¾ cup salsa
- 1 ¼ teaspoon chili powder
- 1 ½ cup rolled oats
- 1 can black beans, rinsed and drained
- 1 tablespoon soy sauce

Directions:

1. In a mixing bowl, combine all ingredients and mix using your hands.
2. Form small patties using your hands and set them aside.
3. Brush patties with oil if desired.
4. Place the grill pan in the air fryer and place the patties on the grill pan accessory.
5. Close the lid and cook for 20 minutes on each side at 330°F.

Nutrition: Calories: 395 Carbs: 52.2g Protein: 24.3g Fat: 5.8g

86. Grilled Cauliflower Steaks

Preparation Time: 10 minutes
Cooking Time: 30 minutes
Serving: 1
L & G Counts : 1 leans ,2 green,1 healthy fat ,5 condiment
Ingredients:

- ½ medium heads cauliflower
- ½ medium shallots, peeled and minced
- Water, as needed
- ½ clove garlic, peeled and minced
- ½ teaspoon ground fennel
- ½ teaspoon minced sage
- ½ teaspoon crushed red pepper flakes
- ½ cup green lentils, rinsed
- ½ cups low-sodium vegetable broth
- Salt, to taste (optional)
- Freshly ground black pepper, to taste
- Chopped parsley, for garnish

Directions:

1. On a flat work surface, cut each of the cauliflower heads in half through the stem, then trim each half, so you get a 1-inch-thick steak.
2. Arrange each piece on a baking sheet and set it aside. You can reserve the extra cauliflower florets for other uses.
3. Sauté the shallots in a medium saucepan over medium heat for 10 minutes, stirring occasionally. Add water, 1 to 3 tablespoons at a time, to keep the shallots from sticking.
4. Stir in the garlic, fennel, sage, red pepper flakes, and lentils, and cook for 3 minutes.
5. Pour into the vegetable broth and bring to a boil over high heat.
6. Reduce the heat to medium, cover, and cook for 30 minutes, or until the lentils are very soft, adding more water as needed.
7. Using an immersion blender, purée the mixture until smooth. Sprinkle with salt (if desired) and pepper. Keep warm and set aside.
8. Preheat the grill to medium heat.
9. Grill the cauliflower steaks for about 7 minutes per side until evenly browned.
10. Transfer the cauliflower steaks to a plate and spoon the purée over them. Serve garnished with parsley.

Nutrition: Calories: 105, Fat: 1.1g, Carbs: 18.3g, Protein: 5.4g, Fiber: 4.9g

87. Beets and Pecans Mix

Preparation Time: 10 minutes
Cooking Time: 20 minutes
Servings: 4
L & G Counts : 0 leans ,0 green,1 healthy fat ,3 condiment
Ingredients:

- 2 cups water
- 1 red onion, sliced
- 4 beets
- 2 tablespoons olive oil
- 2 tablespoons balsamic vinegar
- A pinch salt and black pepper
- 2 tablespoons pecans, chopped

Directions:

1. Add the water to your instant pot, add the steamer basket, add the beets inside, shut the lid, and cook for 20 minutes.
2. Release the pressure naturally for 10 minutes, drain the beets, cool them down, peel, and cut into cubes.
3. In a salad container, combine the beets with the rest of the ingredients, toss, and serve as a side dish.

Nutrition: Calories: 142, Fat: 5 Gram, Carbs: 8g, Protein: 6g

88. Quick Lentil Chili

Preparation Time: 15 minutes
Cooking Time: 30 minutes
Servings: 10
L & G Counts : 0 leans ,1 green,0 healthy fat ,4 condiment
Ingredients:

- 11/2 cups seeded or diced pepper
- 11/2 cups coarsely chopped onions
- 5 cups vegetable broth (it should have a low sodium content)
- 1 tablespoon garlic
- ¼ teaspoon freshly ground pepper
- 1 cup red lentils
- 3 filled teaspoons chili powder
- 1 tablespoon grounded cumin

Directions:

1. Place your pot over medium heat.
2. Combine the onions, red peppers, low sodium vegetable broth, garlic, salt, and pepper in a mixing bowl.
3. Cook, stirring frequently, until the onions are translucent and all of the liquid has evaporated. This should take about 10 minutes.
4. Boil the remaining broth, lime juice, chili powder, lentils, and cumin.
5. Reduce the heat to a simmer and cover for about 10 minutes, or until the lentils are tender. If the mixture appears to be too thick, add a little water.
6. 6. The chili is done when most of the water has been absorbed.
7. Serve and enjoy.

Nutrition: Protein: 2.3 g Carbohydrates: 12.1 g Dietary Fiber: 3.3 g Sugar: 6.1 g Fat: 2.9 g

89. Veggie Red Curry

Preparation Time: 20 minutes
Cooking Time: 30 minutes
Servings: 8
L & G Counts : 0 leans ,2 green,1 healthy fat ,5 condiment
Ingredients:

- 2 tablespoons extra-virgin olive oil
- 1 shallot, chopped
- 4 garlic cloves, minced
- 2 red bell peppers, cored and diced
- 2 carrots, diced
- 1 turnip, peeled and cubed
- 1 parsnip, diced
- 2 sweet potatoes, peeled and cubed
- 1 zucchini, cubed
- ½ pound snow peas
- 1 cup diced tomatoes
- 4 tablespoons red curry paste
- ¼ teaspoon chili powder
- ½ teaspoon cumin powder
- ½ teaspoon ground coriander
- 1 bay leaf
- 1 cup vegetable stock
- Salt and pepper, to taste
- Chopped cilantro, for serving

Directions:

1. Heat the oil in a saucepan and add the shallot, garlic, bell pepper, and carrots. Cook for 5 minutes until softened.
2. Stir in the turnip and the rest of the vegetables, as well as the curry paste, spices, bay leaf, and stock.
3. Adjust the taste with salt and pepper and cover the pot with a lid.
4. Cook on low heat for 30 minutes.
5. Serve the curry warm, sprinkled with freshly chopped cilantro.

Nutrition per serving: Calories: 161 Fat: 6.2g Protein: 3.0g Carbohydrates: 23.9g

90. Spicy Vegetable Noodles

Preparation Time: 19 minutes
Cooking Time: 11 minutes
Servings: 6
L & G Counts : 0 leans ,2 green,1 healthy fat ,3 condiment
Ingredients:

- 12 ounce rice noodles
- 2 tablespoons coconut oil
- 2 garlic cloves, minced
- 1 shallot, sliced
- 1 zucchini, sliced
- 1 red bell pepper, cored and sliced
- 1 teaspoon grated ginger
- 2 cups snow peas
- 1 tablespoon soy sauce
- 1 teaspoon dry sherry

Directions:

1. Fill a pot halfway with water and add the rice noodles. Cook them according to the package directions, then drain thoroughly.
2. In a skillet or frying pan, heat the oil, then add the garlic and shallot. Cook for 1 minute, then add the remaining ingredients and cook for 10 minutes.
3. Remove from the heat and add the rice noodles.
4. Serve the dish hot and hot.

Nutrition per serving: Calories: 149 Fat: 4.9g Protein: 3.2g Carbohydrates: 21.3g

SNACKS

Morning Snacks

91. Super Healthy Green Smoothie

Preparation Time: 10 minutes
Cooking Time: 0 minutes
Servings: 2
L & G Counts : 0 leans ,2 green,0 healthy fat ,3 condiment
Ingredients:

- 1 teaspoon spirulina powder
- 1 cup coconut water
- 2 cups mixed greens
- 1 tablespoon ginger
- 4 tablespoon lemon juice
- 2 celery stalks
- 1 cup cucumber, chopped
- 1 green pear, core removed
- 1 banana

Directions:

1. Add all ingredients to the blender and blend until smooth and creamy.
2. Serve immediately and enjoy.

Nutrition: Calories: 161, Fat: 1, Carbs: 19, Protein: 7 g

92. Chia Seed Smoothie

Preparation Time: 5 minutes
Cooking Time: 0 minutes
Servings: 3
L & G Counts : 0 leans ,1 green,1 healthy fat ,3 condiment
Ingredients:

- ¼ teaspoon Cinnamon
- 1 tablespoon fresh and grated ginger
- Pinch Cardamom
- 1 tablespoon Chia Seeds
- 2 Pitted Medjool Dates
- 1 cup Alfalfa Sprouts
- 1 cup Water
- 1 Banana
- ½ cup unsweetened coconut milk

Directions:

3. Blend everything together until smooth.

Nutrition: Calories: 412   Protein: 18.9g Carbs: 43.8gFat: 24.8g

93. Spinach Peach Banana Smoothie

Preparation Time: 10 minutes
Cooking Time: 0 minutes
Servings: 2
L & G Counts : 0 leans ,2 green,0 healthy fat ,3 condiment
Ingredients:

- 1 cup baby spinach
- 2 cups coconut water
- 1 tablespoon agave syrup
- 2 ripe bananas
- 2 ripe peaches, pitted and chopped

Directions:

1. Add all ingredients to the blender and blend until smooth and creamy.
2. Serve immediately and enjoy.

Nutrition: Calories: 163, Fat: 1, Carbs: 4, Protein: 6

94. Salty Green Smoothie

Preparation Time: 10 minutes
Cooking Time: 0 minutes
Servings: 2
L & G Counts : 0 leans ,2 green,1 healthy fat ,3 condiment
Ingredients:
- 1 cup ice cubes
- ¼ tablespoon liquid aminos
- 1 ½ tablespoon sea salt
- 2 limes, peeled and quartered
- 1 avocado, pitted and peeled
- 1 cup kale leaves
- 1 cucumber, chopped
- 2 cups tomato, chopped
- ¼ cup water

Directions:
1. Add all ingredients to the blender and blend until smooth and creamy.
2. Serve immediately and enjoy.

Nutrition: Calories: 108, Fat: 1, Carbs: 1, Protein: 4

95. Watermelon Kale Smoothie

Preparation Time: 10 minutes
Cooking Time: 0 minutes
Servings: 2
L & G Counts : 0 leans ,1 green,0 healthy fat ,0 condiment
Ingredients:
- 8 ounce water
- 1 orange, peeled
- 3 cups kale, chopped
- 1 banana, peeled
- 2 cups watermelon, chopped
- 1 celery, chopped

Directions:
1. Add all ingredients to the blender and blend until smooth and creamy.
2. Serve immediately and Enjoy.

Nutrition: Calories: 122, Fat: 1, Carbs: 5, Protein: 1

96. Apple Spinach Cucumber Smoothie

Preparation Time: 10 minutes
Cooking Time: 0 minutes
Servings: 1
L & G Counts :0 leans ,3 green,0 healthy fat ,0 condiment
Ingredients:

- ¾ cup water
- ½ green apple, diced
- ¾ cup spinach
- ½ cucumber

Directions:

1. Add all ingredients to the blender and blend until smooth and creamy.
2. Serve immediately and enjoy.

Nutrition: Calories: 90, Fat: 1, Carbs: 21, Protein: 1

97. Refreshing Lime Smoothie

Preparation Time: 10 minutes
Cooking Time: 0 minutes
Servings: 2
L & G Counts : 0 leans ,4 green,0 healthy fat ,4 condiment
Ingredients:

- 1 cup ice cubes
- 20 drops liquid stevia
- 2 fresh lime, peeled and halved
- 1 tablespoon lime zest, grated
- ½ cucumber, chopped
- 1 avocado, pitted and peeled
- 2 cups spinach
- 1 tablespoon creamed coconut
- ¾ cup coconut water

Directions:

1. Add all ingredients to the blender and blend until smooth and creamy.
2. Serve immediately and enjoy.

Nutrition: Calories: 312, Fat: 3, Carbs: 28, Protein: 4

98. Spiced Popcorn

Preparation Time: 5 minutes
Cooking Time: 5 minutes
Servings: 4
L & G Counts : 0 leans ,0 green,1 healthy fat ,3 condiment
Ingredients:

- 3 tablespoons olive oil
- ½ cup popcorn kernels
- Cooking spray
- 1 teaspoon garlic powder
- 1 teaspoon onion powder
- ½ teaspoon smoked paprika
- ½ teaspoon salt
- 1/8 teaspoon cayenne pepper

Directions:

1. Heat the olive oil in the pot. Add three popcorn kernels, and when one pops, add the rest. Cover and shake vigorously until the popcorn is fully popped. Transfer to a large mixing bowl.
2. Cooking spray should be sprayed on the popcorn. Toss the popcorn with clean hands, thoroughly mixing it. Combine the garlic powder, onion powder, paprika, salt, and cayenne pepper in a small bowl. Toss with your preferred spice blend until coated.

Nutrition: Calories: 210, Fat: 17, Carbs: 3, Protein: 16

99. Baked Spinach Chips

Preparation Time: 5 minutes
Cooking Time: 15 minutes
Servings: 4
L & G Counts : 0 leans , 1 green,1 healthy fat ,3 condiment
Ingredients:

- Cooking spray
- 5 ounces baby spinach, washed and patted dry
- 2 tablespoons olive oil
- 1 teaspoon garlic powder
- ½ teaspoon salt
- 1/8 teaspoon freshly ground black pepper

Directions:

3. Preheat the oven to 350°F. Coat 2 baking sheets with cooking spray. Place the spinach in a large bowl. Mix in olive oil, garlic powder, salt, and pepper, and toss until evenly coated.
4. Spread the spinach in a single layer on the baking sheets. Bake until the spinach leaves are crispy and slightly browned. Store spinach chips in a resealable container at room temperature for up to 1 week.

Nutrition: Calories: 451, Fat: 18, Carbs: 7, Protein: 12

100. Peanut Butter Yogurt Dip with Fruit

Preparation Time: 10 minutes
Cooking Time: 5 minutes
Servings: 4
L & G Counts : 0 leans ,0 green,0 healthy fat ,3 condiment
Ingredients:

- 1 cup nonfat vanilla Greek yogurt
- 2 tablespoons natural creamy peanut butter
- 2 teaspoons honey
- 1 pear, cored and sliced
- 1 apple, cored and sliced
- 1 banana, sliced

Directions:

1. In a mixing bowl, combine the yogurt, peanut butter, and honey. Serve the dip alongside the fruit.

Nutrition: Calories: 421, Fat: 5, Carbs: 3, Protein: 10

Afternoon Snacks

101. No-Cook Pistachio-Cranberry Quinoa Bites

Preparation Time: 30 minutes
Cooking Time: 0 minutes
Servings: 12
L & G Counts : 0 leans ,0 green,2 healthy fat ,3 condiment
Ingredients:

- ½ cup quinoa
- ¾ cup natural almond butter
- ¾ cup gluten-free old-fashioned oats
- 2 tablespoons honey
- 1/8 teaspoon salt
- ¼ cup unsalted shelled pistachios, roughly chopped
- ¼ cup dried cranberries

Directions:

1. Blend the quinoa until it turns into a flour consistency. Mix in almond butter, oats, honey and salt, and blend until smooth.
2. Transfer into a medium bowl, and gently fold in the pistachios and cranberries. Spoon out a tablespoon of the batter. Use clean hands to roll into a 2-inch ball and place it into a container. Repeat for the remaining batter, making a total of 12 balls. Let it chill to set.

Nutrition: Calories: 214, Fat: 19, Carbs: 3, Protein: 21

102. Cottage Cheese-Filled Avocado

Preparation Time: 5 minutes
Cooking Time: 3 minutes
Servings: 4
L & G Counts : 0 leans ,0 green,2 healthy fat ,3 condiment
Ingredients:

- ½ cup low-fat cottage cheese
- ¼ cup cherry tomatoes, quartered
- 2 avocados, halved and pitted
- 4 teaspoons pumpkin seeds
- ¼ teaspoon salt
- 1/8 teaspoon freshly ground black pepper

Directions:

1. Mix together the cottage cheese and tomatoes in a bowl. Spoon 2 tablespoons of the cheese-tomato mixture onto each of the avocado halves. Top each with 1 teaspoon of pumpkin seeds, and sprinkle with salt and pepper.

Nutrition: Calories: 212, Fat: 15, Carbs: 3, Protein: 18

103. Toast with Balsamic Glaze

Preparation Time: 5 minutes
Cooking Time: 10 minutes
Servings: 2
L & G Counts : 0 leans ,0 green,0 healthy fat ,3 condiment
Ingredients:

- 1 tablespoon brown sugar
- 5 cherry tomatoes, halved
- 1/8 teaspoon salt
- ½ cup Vinegar
- ½ loaf Bread
- 1/8 teaspoon freshly ground black pepper

Directions:

1. In a hot saucepan, combine the vinegar and brown sugar and stir until dissolved. Bring to a boil and cook until the vinegar thickens. Allow for a 10-minute resting period.
2. Scoop out and mash the pulp into the toast. Season the tomatoes on top. Then drizzle each crouton with the balsamic glaze.

Nutrition: Calories: 214, fat 8, carbs 4, protein 10

104. No-Bake Honey-Almond Granola Bars

Preparation Time: 15 minutes, plus 1 to 2 hours to chill
Cooking Time: 0 minutes
Servings: 8
L & G Counts : 0 leans ,0 green, 2 healthy fat ,3 condiment
Ingredients:

- Cooking spray
- 1 cup pitted dates
- ¼ cup honey
- ¾ cup natural creamy almond butter
- ¾ cup gluten-free rolled oats
- 2 tablespoons raw almonds, chopped
- 2 tablespoons pumpkin seeds

Directions:

1. Line an 8-by-8-inch baking dish with parchment paper, and coat the paper with cooking spray. In a food processor or blender, add the dates and blend until they reach a paste-like consistency. Add the honey, almond butter and oats, and blend until well combined. Transfer the mixture to a medium bowl.
2. Mix almonds and pumpkin seeds, and gently fold until well combined. Fill the baking dish halfway with the mixture. Spread the mixture evenly, using clean fingers to push down the mixture, so it is compact. Let it chill for at least 1 to 2 hours.
3. Take out of the refrigerator and cut into 8 bars. Remove each bar from the baking dish with care and wrap it individually in plastic wrap. Place the bars in the refrigerator until ready to use.

Nutrition: Calories: 121, Fat: 1, Carbs: 8, Protein: 12

105. Whole-Wheat Chocolate-Banana Quesadillas

Preparation Time: 5 minutes
Cooking Time: 5 minutes
Servings: 4
L & G Counts : 0 leans ,0 green,1 healthy fat ,1 condiment
Ingredients:

- Cooking spray
- 2 (10-inch) whole-wheat tortillas
- 1 ½ ounce 60% dark chocolate
- 2 tablespoons natural creamy peanut butter
- 1 medium banana, thinly sliced

Directions:

1. Add a tortilla and warm for 30 seconds on each side in a pan. Melt the chocolate in the microwave, about 1 minute, stirring halfway through. Using a spatula, spread the peanut butter onto 1 tortilla to the edges. Top with the banana slices, and drizzle the chocolate over the peanut butter.
2. Topped with the second tortilla, pressing down gently with the palm of your hand. Cut into 8 pieces and serve.

Nutrition: Calories: 212, Fat: 5, Carbs: 3, Protein: 10

106. Nacho Bites

Preparation Time: 15 minutes
Cooking Time: 10 minutes
Servings: 4
L & G Counts : - leans ,0 green,1 healthy fat ,3 condiment
Ingredients:

- Cooking spray
- ¾ cup low-sodium black beans, drained and rinsed
- ½ teaspoon hot sauce
- ¼ teaspoon salt
- 20 corn tortilla chips
- ½ cup shredded non-dairy cheese

Directions:

1. Preheat the oven to 400°F. Coat 2 baking sheets with cooking spray. Mix and toss beans, hot sauce, and salt. Mash until coarse.
2. Place tortilla chips. Topped the chip with black bean mixture and 1 teaspoon of cheese. Bake until the cheese has melted.

Nutrition: Calories: 290, Fat: 1, Carbs: 3, Protein: 19

107. Cucumber Rolls

Preparation Time: 5 minutes
Cooking Time: 0 minutes
Servings: 6
L & G Counts : 1 leans ,2 green,0 healthy fat ,3 condiment
Ingredients:

- 1 big cucumber, sliced lengthwise
- 1 tablespoon parsley, chopped
- 8 ounce canned tuna, drained and mashed
- Salt and black pepper, to taste
- 1 tsp. lime juice

Directions:

1. Arrange cucumber slices on a work surface, then divide and roll the remaining ingredients.
2. Arrange the rolls as an appetizer on a serving platter.

Nutrition: Calories: 200 Fat: 6 g. Fiber: 3.4 g. Carbs: 7.6 g. Protein: 3.5 g.

108. Olives and Cheese Stuffed Tomatoes

Preparation Time: 10 minutes
Cooking Time: 0 minutes
Servings: 24
L & G Counts : 0 leans ,0 green,1 healthy fat ,3 condiment
Ingredients:

- 24 cherry tomatoes
- 2 tablespoons olive oil
- ¼ teaspoon red pepper flakes
- ½ cup feta cheese, crumbled
- 2 tablespoons black olive paste
- ¼ cup mint

Directions:

1. In a mixing bowl, combine the olive paste and remaining ingredients until smooth (except the cherry tomatoes).
2. Remove the tomato's top and hollow it out.
3. Stuff the cherry tomatoes with the mixture and serve as an appetizer on a serving platter.

Nutrition: Calories: 136 Fat: 8.6 g. Fiber: 4.8 g. Carbs: 5.6 g. Protein: 5.1 g.

109. Tomato and Chives Salsa

Preparation Time: 5 minutes
Cooking Time: 0 minutes
Servings: 6
L & G Counts : 0 leans ,2 green,1 healthy fat ,3 condiment
Ingredients:

- 1 garlic clove, minced
- 4 tablespoon olive oil
- 5 tomatoes, cubed
- 1 tablespoon balsamic vinegar
- ¼ cup basil, chopped
- 1 tablespoon parsley, chopped
- 1 tablespoon chives, chopped
- Salt and black pepper, to taste
- Pita chips, for serving

Directions:

1. Toss the tomatoes with the remaining ingredients (except the pita chips) in a mixing bowl.
2. combine ingredients, divide among bowls, and serve with pita chips on the side.

Nutrition: Calories: 160 Fat: 13.7 g. Fiber: 5.5 g. Carbs: 10.1 g. Protein: 2.2 g.

110. Snickerdoodle Pecans

Preparation Time: 10 minutes
Cooking Time: 15 minutes
Servings: 8
L & G Counts : 0 leans ,0 green,0 healthy fat ,3 condiment
Ingredients:

- Cooking spray
- 1½ cups raw pecans
- 2 tablespoons brown sugar
- 2 tablespoons 100% maple syrup
- ½ teaspoon ground cinnamon
- ½ teaspoon vanilla extract
- 1/8 teaspoon salt

Directions:

1. Line and set the oven to 350°F. In a medium bowl, place the pecans. Add the brown sugar, maple syrup, cinnamon, vanilla and salt, tossing to evenly coat.
2. Place pecans in a single layer. Bake for about 12 minutes, until pecans are lightly browned and fragrant. Remove and set aside for 10 minutes to cool..

Nutrition: Calories: 321, Fat: 28, Carbs: 7, Protein: 42

After-Dinner Snacks

111. Vegan Feta Artichoke Dip

Preparation Time: 10 minutes
Cooking Time: 30 minutes
Servings: 8
L & G Counts : 0 leans ,1 green,1 healthy fat ,1 condiment
Ingredients:

- 8 ounces artichoke hearts, drained and quartered
- ¾ cup basil, chopped
- ¾ cup green olives, pitted and chopped
- 1 cup nondairy cheese, grated
- 5 ounce Vegan feta cheese, crumbled

Directions:

1. In your food processor, mix the artichokes with the basil and the rest of the ingredients, pulse well, and transfer to a baking dish.
2. Put into the oven, bake at 375°F for 30 minutes and serve as a party dip.

Nutrition: Calories: 186; Fat: 12.4 g; Fiber: 0.9 g; Carbs: 2.6 g; Protein: 1.5 g

112. Creamy Raspberry Pomegranate Smoothie

Preparation Time: 5 minutes
Cooking Time: 5 minutes
Serving: 1
L & G Counts : 0 leans ,1 green,0 healthy fat ,3 condiment
Ingredients:

- 1 ½ cups pomegranate juice
- ½ cup unsweetened coconut milk
- 1 scoop vanilla protein powder (plant-based if you need it to be dairy-free)
- 2 packed cups fresh baby spinach
- 1 cup frozen raspberries
- 1 frozen banana
- 1 to 2 tablespoons freshly compressed lemon juice

Directions:

3. In a blender, combine the pomegranate juice and coconut milk. Add the protein powder and spinach. Give these a whirl to break down the spinach.
4. Add the raspberries, banana, and lemon juice, then top it off with ice. Blend until smooth and frothy.

Nutrition: Calories: 303 Total fat: 3g Cholesterol: 0mg Fiber: 2g Protein: 15g Sodium: 165mg

113. Avocado Kale Smoothie

Preparation Time: 5 minutes
Cooking Time: 0 minutes
Servings: 3
L & G Counts : 0 leans ,3 green,1 healthy fat ,1 condiment
Level of Difficulty: Easy
Category: Green/Healthy Fat:
Ingredients:

- 1 cup water
- ½ Seville orange, peeled
- 1 avocado
- 1 cucumber, peeled
- 1 cup kale
- 1 cup ice cubes

Directions:

1. Place all of your ingredients in a blender and blend until smooth and creamy. Serve right away and enjoy.

Nutrition: Calories: 160 Fat: 13.3g Carbs: 11.6g Protein: 2.4g

114. Refreshing Cucumber Smoothie

Preparation Time: 5 minutes
Cooking Time: 0 minutes
Servings: 2
L & G Counts : 0 leans ,2 green,0 healthy fat ,3 condiment
Level of Difficulty: Easy
Category: Green
Ingredients:

- 1 cup ice cubes
- 20 drops liquid stevia
- 2 peeled and halved fresh lime
- 1 teaspoon grated lime zest
- 1 cucumber, chopped
- 1 pitted and peeled avocado
- 2 cups kale
- 1 tablespoon creamed coconut
- ¾ cup coconut water

Directions:

1. Place all of your ingredients in a blender and blend until smooth and creamy.

Serve right away and enjoy. **Nutrition:** Calories: 313 Fat: 25.1g Carbs: 24.7g Protein: 4.9g

115. Soursop Smoothie

Preparation Time: 5 minutes
Cooking Time: 0 minutes
Servings: 2
L & G Counts : 0 leans ,0 green,0 healthy fat ,2 condiment
Level of Difficulty: Easy
Category: Green
Ingredients:

- 3 quartered frozen Burro Bananas
- 1 ½ cups Homemade Coconut Milk
- ¼ cup Walnuts
- 1 teaspoon Sea Moss Gel
- 1 teaspoon ground Ginger
- 1 teaspoon Soursop Leaf Powder
- 1 handful of kale

Directions:

1. Prepare all ingredients and place them in a blender or food processor.
2. Blend until it reaches a smooth consistency. Serve your Soursop Smoothie and enjoy!

Nutrition: Calories: 213 Fat: 3.1g Carbs: 6g Protein: 8g

116. Coconut Smoothie

Preparation Time: 5 minutes
Cooking Time: 0 minutes
Servings: 1
L & G Counts : 1 leans ,0 green,0 healthy fat ,3 condiment
Level of Difficulty: Easy
Category: Healthy Fat:
Ingredients:

- 1 sachet Lean and Green Essential Creamy Vanilla Shake
- 6 ounces unsweetened almond milk
- 6 ounces diet ginger ale
- 2 tablespoons unsweetened coconut, shredded
- ¼ teaspoon rum extract
- ½ cup ice

Directions:

3. In a small blender, place all ingredients and pulse until smooth. Transfer the smoothie into a serving glass and serve immediately.

Nutrition: Calories: 120 Fat: 6.2g Carbs: 15.9g Protein: 15g

117. Black Bean Burgers

Preparation Time: 15 minutes
Cooking Time: 10 minutes
Servings: 8 burgers
L & G Counts : 0 leans ,0 green,1 healthy fat ,4 condiment
Level of Difficulty: Normal
Category: Green
Ingredients:

- ½ cup dried breadcrumbs
- ½ cup sun-dried tomatoes in oil
- 2 tablespoons olive oil
- ½ medium red onion
- 1 tablespoon paprika
- 1 ½ tablespoon cumin
- ½ tablespoon salt
- 1 can black beans
- 1 egg
- ½ cup rolled oats

Directions:

1. Wash and drain the black beans. Blend with a hand blender and place it in a big mixing bowl. Conversely, crush the beans with a fork/masher.
2. Dice the red onion and sundried tomatoes, and add them to the dish. Then, add some salt, chickens, cumin, oats, paprika, olive oil, etc. Give a nice stir to it.
3. Finally, put some of the breadcrumbs until you're left with a good, firm mixture. It's fine if you don't need all of the breadcrumbs. Sculpt the paste into patties for burgers. If it is too sticky, wet your hands a little.
4. Fry in a pan with a little oil, or place on a grill. Cook on both sides within 5 minutes, turning occasionally. Serve whatever you fancy with your favorite burger ingredients: a bun, lettuce, tomato, cheese!

Nutrition: Calories: 95 Carbs: 18g Fat: 1g Protein: 6g

118. Lean and Green Smoothie

Preparation Time: 5 minutes
Cooking Time: 0 minutes
Servings: 1
L & G Counts : 0 leans ,2 green,0 healthy fat ,3 condiment
Ingredients:

- 2 ½ cups kale leaves
- ¾ cup chilled apple juice
- 1 cup cubed pineapple
- ½ cup frozen green grapes
- ½ cup chopped apple

Directions:

1. In a blender, combine the pineapple, apple juice, apple, frozen seedless grapes, and kale leaves.
2. Cover and mix until smooth.
3. When the smoothie is finished, garnish with halved grapes if desired.

Nutrition: Calories: 81 Protein: 2 g Carbohydrates: 19 g Fat: 1 g

119. Tropical Greens Smoothie

Preparation Time: 5 minutes
Cooking Time: 5 minutes
Servings: 1
L & G Counts : 0 leans ,4 green,0 healthy fat ,3 condiment
Ingredients:

- 1 banana
- ½ peeled and segmented large navel orange
- ½ cup frozen mango chunks
- 1 cup frozen spinach
- 1 celery stalk, broken into pieces
- 1 tablespoon cashew or almond butter
- ½ tablespoon spiraling
- ½ tablespoon ground flaxseed
- ½ cup nonda iry milk, unsweetened
- Water, for thinning (optional)

Directions:

1. Combine the bananas, orange, mango, spinach, celery, cashew butter, spiraling (if using), flaxseed, and milk in a high-speed blender or food processor.
2. Blend until smooth, adding more milk or water as needed to thin if the smoothie is too thick. Serve immediately — it tastes best when it's hot.

Nutrition: Calories: 391 Fat: 12 g Protein: 13 g Carbohydrates: 68 g Fiber: 13 g

120. Cocoa Brownies

Preparation Time: 10 minutes.
Cooking Time: 30 minutes.
Servings: 12.
L & G Counts : 1 leans ,0 green,0 healthy fat ,3 condiment
Ingredients:

- 1 egg.
- 2 tablespoons vegan butter, grass-fed.
- 2 teaspoons vanilla extract, pure.
- ¼ teaspoon baking powder.
- ¼ cup cocoa powder.
- 1/3 cup heavy cream.
- ¾ cup almond butter.
- Pinch sea salt.

Directions:

3. Break your egg into a bowl, whisking until smooth.
4. Add in all of your wet ingredients, mixing well.
5. Mix all dry ingredients into a bowl.
6. Sift your dry ingredients into your wet ingredients, mixing to form a batter.
7. Use a baking pan, greasing it before pouring in your mixture.
8. Preheat the oven to 350 degrees Fahrenheit and bake for 25 minutes.
9. Allow it to cool before slicing and serve at room temperature or warm.

Nutrition: Calories: 184. Protein: 1 g. Fat: 20 g. Carbohydrates: 1 g.

Shopping List

Meat

- Boneless, skinless chicken breasts
- Skinless, boneless chicken tenders
- Turkey breast
- Ground turkey
- Extra-lean ground turkey
- Flank steak
- Ground pork
- Salmon
- Grouper
- Shrimp
- Scallops

Egg & Dairy

- Eggs
- Unsalted butter
- Low-fat plain yogurt
- Low-fat plain Greek yogurt
- Light sour cream
- Whipped cream
- Whipped topping
- Low-fat cream cheese
- Strawberry-flavored light cream cheese
- Low-fat cheddar cheese
- Cottage cheese
- Low-fat Mexican cheese
- Low-fat Parmesan cheese
- Part-skim ricotta cheese
- Fresh mozzarella cheese

Fruit

- Apple
- Orange
- Fresh strawberries
- Avocados
- Canned peaches

Vegetables & Fresh Herbs

- Zucchini
- Broccoli
- Cauliflower
- Fresh mushrooms
- Fresh button mushrooms
- Asparagus
- Red bell peppers
- Yellow bell pepper
- Green bell pepper
- Fresh kale
- Fresh baby kale
- Fresh spinach

- Fresh baby spinach
- Carrots
- Frozen peas
- Celery stalks
- Tomatoes
- Cherry tomatoes
- Cucumber
- Radishes
- Scallions
- Onion
- Garlic
- Fresh ginger

- Lettuce
- Jalapeño pepper
- Pepperoni pepper
- Lime
- Lemon
- Fresh chives
- Fresh parsley
- Fresh rosemary
- Fresh mint
- Fresh cilantro
- Fresh thyme
- Fresh basil

Seasoning & Dried Herbs

- Salt
- Ground cinnamon
- Ground nutmeg
- Ground cumin
- Cayenne pepper
- Red pepper flakes
- Red chili powder
- Ground black pepper
- Garlic salt

- Garlic powder
- Pumpkin pie spice
- Taco seasoning
- Curry powder
- Curry paste
- Dried parsley
- Dried thyme
- Dried oregano

Extra:

- Olive oil cooking spray
- Olive oil
- Extra-virgin olive oil
- Coconut oil
- Vegetable oil

- Sesame oil
- Unsweetened almond milk
- Unsweetened cashew milk
- Diet ginger ale
- Tahini

- Chili garlic sauce
- Low-sodium soy sauce
- Fish sauce
- Hot sauce
- Hot buffalo sauce
- Sriracha
- White vinegar
- Balsamic vinegar
- Marshmallow dip
- Sugar:-free caramel syrup
- Sugar:-free pancake syrup
- Sugar:-free chocolate syrup
- Honey
- Maple syrup
- Stevia powder
- Zero-calorie sugar substitute
- Splenda
- Splenda with Fiber
- Baking powder
- Unsweetened cocoa powder
- Coffee powder
- Instant espresso powder
- Arrowroot starch
- Ground flaxseed

- Chia seeds
- Dijon mustard
- Peanut butter powder
- Vanilla extract
- Almond extract
- Rum extract
- Peppermint extract
- Egg liquid substitute
- Egg beaters
- 100% canned pumpkin
- Pumpkin puree
- Sugar:-free tomato sauce
- Sugar:-free tomato paste
- Low-sodium chicken broth
- Low-sodium vegetable broth
- Tofu
- Extra-firm tofu
- Tempeh
- Pine nuts
- Almonds
- Pumpkin seeds
- Unsweetened coconut
- Green food coloring

Fueling Hacks Products

- Double Chocolate Brownie Mix
- Wild Blueberry Almond Hot Cereal
- Blueberry Almond Hot Cereal

- Essential Creamy Vanilla Shake
- Essential Honey Mustard & Onion Sticks
- Chia Bliss Smoothie

- Essential Cinnamon Crunchy Oat Cereal
- Essential Velvety Hot Chocolate
- Oatmeal raisin crunch bar
- Oatmeal
- Mashed Potatoes
- Essential Smashed Potatoes
- Brownie Mix
- Puffed Sweet & salty Snacks
- Sharp Cheddar & Sour Cream popcorn
- Golden Pancake
- Olive Oil & Sea Salt Popcorn
- Chicken Noodle Soup
- Cream of Tomato Soup
- Essential Spiced Gingerbread
- Essential Decadent Double Brownie
- Essential Chocolate Chip Pancakes
- Brownie Mix
- Peanut Butter Chocolate Crunch Bar
- Hearty Red Bean & Vegetable Chili
- Essential Red Berry Crunch O's Cereal
- Essential Chocolate Chip Cookie
- Honey Sweet Potatoes
- Essential Frosty Mint Chocolate Soft Serve Treat
- Chocolate Cherry Ganache Bar
- Buttermilk Cheddar Herb Biscuit
- Select Cheddar Herb Biscuit
- Essential Creamy Double Peanut Butter Crisp Bar
- Essential Golden Chocolate Chip Pancakes
- Yogurt Berry Blast Smoothie
- Essential Caramel Macchiato Shake
- Olive Oil & Sea Salt Popcorn
- Dark Chocolate Covered Cherry Shake
- French Vanilla Shake
- Chocolate Chip Pancakes
- Parmesan Cheese Puffs, crushed finely
- Meal Mixed Berry Cereal Crunch
- Cinnamon Pretzel Sticks
- Macaroni & Cheese
- Chocolate pudding
- Chocolate shake
- Calorie Burn Cappuccino
- Maple Brown Sugar: Oatmeal
- Mixed Berry Flavor Infuser
- Brownie
- Cappuccino mix
- Chocolate Chip Pancakes
- S'more Crunch Bar

Conclusion

I know you're the kind of person who constantly balances things: work, kids, housework, hobbies. You take care of everyone else, but you find yourself feeling drained and short of time to enjoy life. At first, it seems like nothing changes or improves, even if you are working hard. But what if I told you that there is a way to eat delicious food that tastes better than anything you've ever eaten before and save money? It is true, this cookbook was designed with you in mind! This book will show you how to buy cheaper ingredients by shopping at local farmers' markets or buying from wholesale clubs like Costco or Sam's Club. You will be amazed at how much food you have for the money! You will also learn how to prepare and store dishes that taste better than restaurant food, throwing out only the leftovers. You will feel proud of yourself when you look in the mirror knowing that your family is being fed well while you are saving money.

I'm sure you're curious about how much this book will cost you. You're not the type of person who believes in spending a lot of money on food, but that doesn't mean you don't want to spend next to nothing. You want to get the most out of your money while eating delicious food. My goal was to make this book as accessible as possible so that you can read it and feel good about acquiring a healthier lifestyle for your family without

Break the bank. So, what do you say? Will you join me on my healthy culinary adventure this year? I am sure you will like it and would love to know all about your delicious discoveries while you save.

In this Lean and Green cookbook, we've covered tons of ways to save money on your grocery bill, as well as tricks for turning simple dishes into healthy miracles. There are all kinds of recipes, cheap, quick and complex for cooking lovers to make. And you don't have to be a chef to make them!

Many of the recipes in this cookbook will give you the opportunity to eat tasty, guilt-free food. You'll get all the nutrients your body needs every day and it won't have all those extra calories - you don't need. Don't have these extra calories - it will help you with your weight loss efforts or other weight-related goals, and this book can serve as one of your tools as you work towards achieving them.

You will begin to feel better as you learn to include these foods in your diet and enjoy your best looks thanks to your healthier choices. You will find that surviving on both a lean and green diet can be a lot easier than you ever imagined. In this book, you can find all kinds of delicious recipes designed to benefit you and your body in so many different ways. Many of the recipes in this cookbook are very healthy, but others are just for fun, which means there's something for everyone.

To experiment with new ingredients, I cook a lot. Anyone who shares my passion knows that the kitchen is my favorite room in the house. Cooking makes me happy, it's relaxing and fun. If you don't feel like cooking alone, invite your friends (or your significant other) to join you - it'll be a lot more fun! No diet can survive without a healthy dose of variety in the dishes you eat.

There's no need to eat the same thing every day, just browse your favorite cookbooks and pick out some new dishes to try. You and your family will love these new recipes and can save you time and money in the process.

Made in the USA
Monee, IL
27 May 2024

59015219R00052